WALL STREET 1920-1970

Five Fabulous Decades

"I just don't understand you, Harry. Everything I've ever read says you're supposed to buy stocks when they're low and sell them when they're high."

WALL STREET 1920-1970

Five Fabulous Decades

HARLAND W. HOISINGTON, Sr.

VANTAGE PRESS

New York Washington Hollywood

FIRST EDITION

Published by Vantage Press, Inc.
516 West 34th Street, New York, N.Y. 10001

Manufactured in the United States of America

Standard Book No. 533-00244-3

FOR HELEN

MY LOVELY, LOYAL WIFE,
WHO HAS TOLERATED ME FOR MORE
THAN FIFTY-THREE YEARS.

"Got anything that's moving fast? I don't have time for the waiting game."

PREFACE

My original motivation in undertaking this book was to relate some of the more interesting experiences I have had while advising clients during this fabulous fifty-year period. As work progressed, historical events were increasingly noted and incorporated because they had a direct bearing on the stock and bond markets.

In the end result, although I have certainly overlooked a few, I believe the story touches on a broad spectrum of the important events of the past five decades, a period which encompassed ten Presidential terms. Against this historical backdrop, I hope to have conveyed the investment hopes, fears, successes and failures of several decades of investors – as reflected in the marketplace – in addition to my role as counselor to some of them. The amount of monies placed under my supervision over these years has been approximately $500,000,000.

Bernard Baruch once made the comment, "My advice to investors who cannot give full time to a study of investments is to seek out some trusted Investment Counselor. The emergence of this new profession of disinterested investment analysts, who have no allegiances and whose only job is to judge a security on its merits, is one of the most constructive and healthy developments of the last half century."

My years in the profession have been both rewarding and challenging. I would most certainly recommend it to a young man today interested in a career in the investment field as the soundest, fairest way to provide professional advice. The wealth of this nation is unbelievable, and our wealth – in spite of high taxes and sporadic interruptions in growth – is increasing rapidly. Since there are more and more people in need of Investment Counsel, the opportunities are unlimited, providing one is properly trained and equipped.

It is not an easy profession. It requires concentration on current events and economic developments, and on changing times and conditions. Perhaps most important to develop is the ability to sift through the myriad statistics and written material available on securities and perceive *quality* in making one's investment choices. But I would not trade – even for IBM at $10 – my fifty-two years of Investment Counseling and the rich, amusing and rewarding experiences they have afforded me.

ACKNOWLEDGMENTS

The author gratefully acknowledges permission to use material from the following sources.

David L. Babson & Co., Inc., Boston, for material from *The Weekly Staff Letter*.

John Brooks for the quotation from *Once in Golconda*.

Chicago Tribune for the use of articles on John Nichols.

The Commercial and Financial Chronicle, New York, for passages from the *Chronicle*.

Dow Jones and Company, New York, for material from articles in *The Wall Street Journal,* and for the use of the Dow Jones Averages which are owned by Dow Jones and Company, publishers of *The Wall Street Journal*.

First National City Bank, New York, for material from their *Monthly Economic Letter* and for the stock ratings for 1927, 1928, and 1929.

Robert Goldston for quotations from *The Great Depression,* published by Bobbs Merrill Co., Inc.

Houghton Mifflin Company, Boston, for material from *The Gathering Storm* by Winston Churchill and from *Ambassador's Journal* by John Kenneth Galbraith.

Moody's Investors Service, Inc., New York, for the charts on Dow Jones Averages from 1929 to the present.

George P. Rhodes for use of the information about his family.

John L. Spivak for the quotations from *A Man in His Time,* published by Horizon Press, New York.

Standard and Poor's Corporation, New York, for use of the chart: Stock Market History Since 1926, and for information on American Tel and Tel, New York Central RR, U.S. Steel, Radio Corporation of America and General Electric Co.

The New York Times and Gimbel's, New York, for use of the poem "Ever Since Adam and Eve"; and for excerpt from "Long-Standing Wall St. Fears Fulfilled as a Big Broker Fails" —*New York Times,* Sunday edition of March 15, 1970; excerpt from "When Wall Street Catches the Flu, 26 Million Americans Ache" by Charles J. Rolo, in *The New York Times Magazine* of August 31, 1969; Editorial "The Shrinking Dollar" of September 23, 1969.

In addition, I wish to thank the following people for encouragement and assistance:

Carlos Baker for taking time to read the manuscript and for his helpful suggestions;

V. Orval Watts for his assistance and encouragement;

James W. Wooster, Jr., who was extremely helpful and cooperative;

Frank Rathje, who provided information on the Bank Holiday;

Firestone Library of Princeton University, from which I received pertinent information;

American Telephone & Telegraph Co.;

General Motors Corporation, and

Radio Corporation of America.

And others:

Mrs. Robert E. Cooper, Jr. (Catherine), who gave me excellent suggestions in selecting a name for the book, as well as access to her library in Sea Girt, New Jersey; and

My efficient and loyal secretaries, Mrs. Grace Metz, Mrs. Margaret Benedict, and Miss Barbara Clare.

Princeton University Press, Lansing Collins: ***Princeton Past and Present*** (*Re:* Nassau Street)

THE DOW-JONES INDUSTRIAL AVERAGE

This Average has been widely used for over forty years by most followers of the stock market – news commentators, securities analysts, and individual investors. Because of this broad acceptance, I have elected to quote and refer to it as a "measure of the market" through the decades discussed.

A brief history of how this Average was conceived and the main purpose it serves should be useful. Dow Jones and Company began the daily publication of *average closing prices* of active industrial stocks on October 7, 1896. Twelve stocks were used until 1916, when the list was increased to twenty and the new Average figured retroactively back to December, 1914. On October 1, 1928, the list was enlarged to thirty stocks, where it has remained since, although substitutions among the components have been made from time to time. Although both Utility and Transportation Averages have also been incorporated and figured daily by Dow Jones and Company, it is the *Industrial Average* people refer to when they ask, "How is the market?"

Its purpose is to give a *general* rather than a precise idea of the fluctuations in the securities markets, and to reflect the historical continuity of security price movements. When the Dow-Jones Industrial Average drops twenty points from, say, 900, some people will likely say, "the market has fallen out of bed." But of course, it has done nothing of the sort. A twenty-point decline from 900 is only fractionally more than two percent. If an individual stock priced at $50 fell two percent, it would only go down one dollar. A ten-point rise in the Average from the 900 level would be only a little more than one percent – comparable to a fifty-cent rise in the $50 stock.

The thirty stocks presently composing the Industrial Average include:

Allied Chemical	General Electric
Aluminum Co. of America	General Foods
American Can	General Motors

American Telephone
American Brands
Anaconda
Bethlehem Steel
Chrysler Corp.
E. I. du Pont de Nemours
Eastman Kodak
Goodyear
International Harvester
International Nickel
International Paper
Johns-Manville
Owens-Illinois
Procter & Gamble
Sears, Roebuck
Standard Oil (Calif.)
Standard Oil (N. J.)
Swift & Co.
Texaco
Union Carbide
United Aircraft
U. S. Steel
Westinghouse Electric
F. W. Woolworth

No Average can possibly reflect the movement of all stocks. As of year's end, 1970, there were 1789 stocks on the New York Stock Exchange, another 1088 on the American Exchange, and over 11,000 traded actively over-the-counter and not on either national exchange. Many are going up while others are going down – at any time. But the "Dow Jones" at least gives us a feel for their direction.

THE DOW-JONES INDUSTRIAL AVERAGE

Yearly Highs and Lows

Year	*High*	*Low*
1897	55.82	38.49
1898	60.97	42.00
1899	77.61	60.41
1900	71.04	52.96
1901	77.08	61.52
1902	68.44	59.57
1903	67.70	42.15
1904	73.23	46.41
1905	96.56	68.76
1906	103.00	85.18
1907	96.37	53.00
1908	87.67	58.62
1909	100.53	79.91
1910	98.34	73.62
1911	87.06	72.94
1912	94.15	80.15
1913	88.57	72.11
1914	83.43	71.42
1915	99.21	54.22
1916	110.15	84.96
1917	99.18	65.95
1918	89.07	73.38
1919	119.62	79.15
1920	109.88	66.75
1921	81.50	63.90
1922	103.43	78.59
1923	105.38	85.76
1924	120.51	88.33
1925	159.39	115.00
1926	166.64	135.20
1927	202.40	152.73
1928	300.00	191.33
1929	381.17	198.69
1930	294.07	157.51
1931	194.36	73.79
1932	88.78	41.22
1933	108.67	50.16
1934	110.74	85.51
1935	148.44	96.71
1936	184.90	143.11
1937	194.40	113.64
1938	158.41	98.95
1939	155.92	121.44
1940	152.80	111.84
1941	133.59	106.34
1942	119.71	92.92
1943	145.82	119.26
1944	152.53	134.22
1945	195.82	151.35
1946	212.50	163.12
1947	186.85	163.21
1948	193.16	165.39
1949	200.52	161.60
1950	235.47	196.81
1951	276.37	238.99
1952	292.00	256.35
1953	293.79	255.49
1954	404.39	279.87
1955	488.40	388.20
1956	521.05	462.35
1957	520.77	419.79
1958	583.65	436.89
1959	679.36	574.46
1960	685.47	566.05
1961	734.91	610.25
1962	726.01	535.76
1963	767.21	646.79
1964	891.71	766.08
1965	969.26	840.59
1966	995.15	744.32
1967	943.08	786.41
1968	985.21	825.13
1969	968.85	769.93
1970	850.00	631.11

CONTENTS

PART FOUR: 1950-1960

PART FIVE: 1960-1970

PART ONE

1920-1930

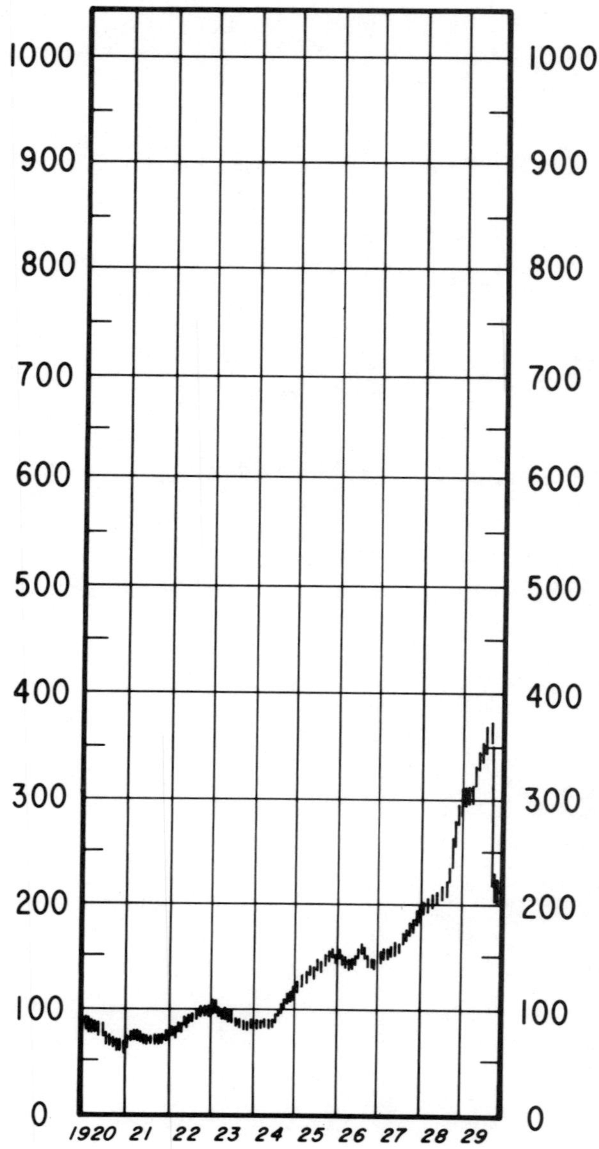
1000
900
800
700
600
500
400
300
200
100
0
1920 21 22 23 24 25 26 27 28 29

CHAPTER ONE

WEST VIRGINIA – A BEGINNING

I entered this vocation more through luck than planning. My wife, Helen, and I were married in 1918, during World War I. I was fortunate in being discharged from Naval Aviation in December of 1918. Jobs were very scarce and although I had an A. B. Degree from Ohio University, I had not specialized in any particular field. My majors had been Economics, Accounting, and Money and Banking because I had a genuine interest in these areas.

A friend of ours was associated with the Philadelphia office of an excellent Boston investment firm. He was doing well and suggested that I might like the financial field. I expressed interest and, one day in the summer of 1919, went in to meet the managing partner. He apparently liked me and said that with a few months' training I could qualify for a job with them covering West Virginia. I felt confident that I would enjoy the profession and jobs were very scarce, so I accepted the assignment. The starting salary was fairly low. In July, 1920, after a few months of training, I bravely set out for Huntington,West Virginia ,with Helen and our young son. In studying the map of West Virginia and on making inquiries, Huntington seemed to be the most focal point.

Many of my readers may not realize the vast changes that have occurred in our nation during my subsequent fifty-year career. A pause to consider some of them would be timely.

1920	*1970*
Population: 90,000,000	205,000,000
Gross National Product: $70,000,000,000	1,050,000,000,000
National Debt: $3,000,000,000	$385,000,000,000
Telephones: 12,668,000	116,000,000
Automobiles: 7,500,000	112,000,000
Income Taxes: negligible	30 to 70%
Radios: a few headphones	340,000,000
Television: none	95,000,000
Commercial airlines: none	40
Number of stockholders: estimated 500,000	30,850,000

I remember when women's suffrage was granted in 1920, incorporated in the Constitution as the Nineteenth Amendment: "The right of citizens of the United States to vote shall not be denied or abridged by the United States, or any state, on account of sex."

Later in the same year there occurred the famous bomb incident at J. P. Morgan's office on Wall Street at Broad. According to witnesses, shortly before 12:00 noon on September 16, 1920, a horse and wagon driven by one man was seen going west on Wall Street. When the vehicle reached a point directly opposite J. P. Morgan's office, a tremendous explosion occurred, breaking virtually every window in the immediate vicinity. Pandemonium followed and the entire front of the Morgan building was pockmarked by small shrapnel-like iron slugs. Fragments of glass fell to the banking floor, but fortunately no deaths occurred in the Morgan office. The New York Stock Exchange, a block away, was the scene of chaos. Brokers, traders, specialists, clerks all crowded to the center of the room, hoping to avoid flying glass, and the Exchange was closed immediately. In a matter of minutes, reportedly 10,000 people were at the scene, and during the day, 30,000. It was determined that thirty persons had been killed and several hundred badly injured. Total property damage reached several million. Injuries and deaths would have been much greater, but fortunately hundreds of clerks and office boys had already left many of the buildings for an early lunch.

The culprit or culprits of this heinous crime were never identified. For several years, local and federal police conducted an extensive and prolonged investigation, but no tangible evidence was ever uncovered that would point to the guilty person or persons responsible. There was little doubt about the explosives being carried in the horse and wagon. The horse, the driver, and the vehicle were blown to bits – so much so that it was impossible to find anything that could be used as source for identification.

Probably the most important event of 1920 was the election of Warren G. Harding as our twenty-ninth President. He defeated the Democratic candidate, former Governor James M. Cox of Ohio, by a large margin. Even more surprising, he conducted his campaign from a rocking chair on the front porch of his house in Marion, Ohio. Harding had been a senator from that state, was quite handsome and at the time was thought to have a clean record. He proved to be one of the weakest Presidents ever to enter the White House. He surrounded himself with inferior and unscrupulous men, such as Attorney General Harry M. Daugherty from Ohio and Secretary of the Interior Albert B. Fall. In

1915, President Woodrow Wilson had set aside an area near Casper, Wyoming known as "Teapot Dome" as an oil reserve for the U. S. Navy. Later, President Harding transferred control from the Navy to the Department of the Interior. In 1922, Secretary Fall leased to Harry F. Sinclair – without competitive bidding – the Teapot Dome fields. In 1923, Senator Thomas J. Walsh conducted a Senate investigation of this transfer of property. Fall resigned his cabinet post and the investigation led to criminal prosecutions under which Fall was convicted of accepting bribes, sentenced to a year in prison, and fined $100,000. The oil fields were subsequently restored to the U.S. Government through a Supreme Court decision in 1927.

Harding was said to have admitted publicly that he was not qualified for the Presidency. In 1923, he died suddenly and mysteriously in San Francisco on his way home from a trip to Alaska.

As history knows, he was succeeded by his Vice-President, Calvin Coolidge, of Vermont. Coolidge rose to public prominence in 1919, when Governor of Massachusetts. Boston police went on strike and Coolidge immediately and with courage called out the militia and the strike was short-lived. For this he received great acclaim.

Coolidge was an honest but extremely conservative man, and not capable of meeting the problems that confronted the nation. He was reelected in 1924, but in 1928 made the famous statement, "I do not choose to run."

During the years 1920, 1921, 1922 and part of 1923, I was working assiduously in West Virginia and I had some exciting and fascinating experiences. Booker T. Washington once said, "I have learned that success is to be measured not so much by the position that one has reached in life as by the obstacles which he has overcome while trying to succeed." At this point I shall not attempt to enumerate all the obstacles confronting me, but a few are in order.

Farm prices declined precipitately in 1920–1921.

The Florida land boom collapsed in 1926 and millions of dollars were lost by investors.

Interest rates were very high; investors were cautious and reluctant to buy.

There was rampant inflation abroad, particularly in Germany and France. In Germany the mark became valueless and it was said that in 1923 a German worker could not buy a single egg with one month's salary.

With this background I started my new job in West Virginia.

I did not know a soul in the state. Years before, our Ohio University football team had played West Virginia University at Morgantown as well as Marshall College in Huntington. These were the only two times I had ever set foot on West Virginia soil.

Fortunately or unfortunately rail was the only form of travel, with few minor exceptions. Hard surfaced roads were rare. Even if good roads had existed, we were much too poor to afford a car. In the southern part of the state the C.&O., Norfolk and Western and the Virginian Railway were available; if one wanted to go north he used the B.&O. Often I would leave Huntington early Monday morning (the railroad officials seemed to have gone to great efforts to have trains leave about 6:00 a.m.) and would not return until Friday.

As far as my profession was concerned, West Virginia was Virgin Soil. In fact, I was the first investment man to invade the state. I knew that I had to produce some results fairly soon or my job would be in jeopardy. In addition to my salary, my expense account would run $150 to $200 per month. So I threw all of my ingenuity and energy into the task and Helen stood by me through some dark moments.

There was great wealth in the state but it was scattered and not easy to find. My first step was to obtain an Ohio University catalogue and locate any alumni in the state. There were not too many, and of the ones that appeared a number were schoolteachers or in professions that would indicate little wealth.

Soon I had a real break and capitalized on it immediately. I found an alumnus, some twenty years older than I, who was a senior officer in one of the largest banks in Charleston. Fortunately, he was a fraternity brother as well. I immediately took the C.&O. and had a very nice reception from this gentleman. He proved to be warm, personable and prepared to help struggling young men. I explained who I was, told him something about my firm, and what my mission was. He said, "Harland, you are just the man West Virginia needs and as far as I know you have no competition." Within three months his bank became a client.

It developed that he had been in this bank for twenty years, was popular, highly regarded, and knew most of the important people in southern West Virginia. He asked, of course, that I not use his name, but told me of three of the wealthiest men in the area, all located in Raleigh County and living within a radius of ten miles of each other – one in Glen Jean, one in Oak Hill and the third in Mt. Hope. Without wasting time I took the C.&O. to Thurmond and then a bus for about ten miles to Glen Jean, my first stop. Here I received the coolest reception imaginable. The gentleman, as events later proved, was actually a cultured, well-educated bachelor, and the two of us eventually became great friends. But on my first call he was as cold as a cake of ice, and after a cursory and firm "no interest" I had to withdraw – very discouraged. His office, incidentally, was in the rear of a bank of which he was president and controlling stockholder. In it were a very plain oak desk, two or three chairs, and no rugs.

On my return to Huntington I stopped in Charleston and reported the results of my trip to my friend. His reply was, "Harland, this man needs you so don't give up. He will eventually show some interest. I have known him for twenty years and it was only recently that he called me by my first name." Then he asked me how I had made out in Oak Hill and Mt. Hope. I replied that I had had a cordial and warm reception with both men and expected them to become clients. Both of them did (I think my Charleston friend helped), and were wonderful clients for several years.

But not so with my friend in Glen Jean. The second, third, and fourth visits were unsuccessful, but on the fifth there were signs of interest. These trips were made at monthly intervals. At our sixth meeting I could see definite signs of encouragement. When I went into his office, he looked up at me – he was a handsome man with great bushy eyebrows and looked very much like John L. Lewis – and said, "Mr. Hoisington, where are you having supper tonight?" I said that I expected to spend the night in Mt. Hope and to dine there at the hotel. He inquired, "Will you have supper with me?" I was overjoyed and quickly accepted. He picked up his phone, called his house, and told his housekeeper, "Put another potato in the pot, I am bringing a gentleman to dinner."

Although one of West Virginia's wealthiest men, he lived in a modest frame house across the street from the bank and did not even own an automobile at that time. Once in his house, one saw definite evidence of culture and refinement. His library contained many beautiful and rare books and it was obvious that he was an educated, scholarly man.

After supper we returned to the library for coffee. Finally, he said, "Young man, I like you and I would like to do business with you." He was a client for many years and an exceptionally nice one. He died several years ago, as did my clients in Oak Hill and Mt. Hope. I was only about twenty-four when I met them, and they were all mature men of fifty-five to sixty years of age.

With the help of my Charleston friend, and later with that of a very well-to-do young man in Huntington who played football with me at Ohio University, I was able within two years to build up a very nice business. My firm was elated, and so was I. There were two clients in

Charleston, four in Raleigh County, two in Hinton (near White Sulphur), two in Logan, one in Clarksburg and three in Huntington. Several of these clients were banks, and most of them sizable accounts.

I had studied the state carefully in an attempt to locate the wealthiest communities, and this eventually led me to Bluefield. It was an overnight ride from Huntington on the Norfolk and Western. In 1920 sleeping cars were still anything but modern and comfortable. In order to economize I always took an upper berth. The N. & W. between Huntington and Bluefield contains probably some of the crookedest railroad tracks in the nation, with many tunnels. The road was built primarily to haul coal, and passenger trains were of secondary importance. It was a rough and uncomfortable trip. We arrived in Bluefield at 6:00 a.m. (even arrivals seemed to be planned for an ungodly hour). I went to the hotel, had some breakfast, and at nine o'clock went forth to call on the banks. I had learned that banks were prospective clients – they really needed professional guidance in those days. If I failed to interest the bank as a client, I always asked for its latest statement, and in this way obtained the names of all the directors. It was pretty safe to assume that they would be the wealthiest and most influential men in the community. We can forget Bluefield, however, because for some unknown reason I could never, after several attempts, break the ice there. To be facetious I left Bluefield rather blue.

CHAPTER TWO

WELCH, AND THE HATFIELD-McCOY FEUD

I learned that Welch, located between Bluefield and Huntington in McDowell County, had considerable wealth. Consulting a timetable, I found that the Norfolk and Western had a train leaving Bluefield at 4:00 p.m., arriving in Welch at 6:00 p.m. – so I promptly purchased a ticket for my first visit to Welch.

It was a typical coal town, with one very second-grade hotel situated directly across the street from the railroad station. (Try to imagine the noise from the N.&W. 100-car coal trains, powered by two huge steam engines, passing in the night.) I was preceded to the hotel by about ten traveling salesmen. As I stood last in line the proprietor greeted each patron with the expression, "Horses Off." Most of them replied in kind, but I noticed that a few of them failed to respond. Not knowing what this expression implied, I remained silent, but soon learned its meaning. A reply meant that you were an old patron and were given a room in the main hotel – which was anything but luxurious. If one failed to respond, he was exiled to the horrible frame annex around the corner, across the street from the courthouse.

I wish I had words to describe the annex adequately. It was an ugly, dirty, two-story frame building. Windows were so encrusted that one could scarcely see through them. My room was at the front of the building on the second floor. It contained an old iron bed with a thin mattress over some very ancient springs. The only other furniture were a washstand with a pitcher of water, a wash basin, and in the lower part, a chamber. Down a dark, dingy hall at the rear of the building there was a flush toilet – if one preferred this to the chamber. I went over to the main hotel for dinner, where the meal was anything but exotic, then returned to my room and went to bed (what else could one do?). I had been up and working since six o'clock in the morning, and was weary. Despite the uncomfortable bed, I slept soundly.

Shortly after daybreak I was awakened by gunfire that seemed to be just under my window. I knew from the sound and the rapidity of the shots that it was something serious. I jumped out of bed and ran to the window to see a horrible sight. The body of a man was rolling down the courthouse steps followed by two men, each with a six-shooter, who pumped lead into the body until it reached the bottom of the steps. I didn't realize it then, but I was witnessing one of the most famous killings of the century. When the shooting had stopped and I had caught my breath and regained my composure, I dressed quickly and went downstairs to find out who was shot and why. By this time a great crowd had gathered in front of the courthouse. Two bodies were lying there, surrounded by the curious crowd. I heard one man say, "Well, they finally got old Sid." I learned later that old Sid was the one and only Sid Hatfield of the famous Hatfield–McCoy feud.

> The Hatfield–McCoy feud is probably the most famous in American folklore. There were two clans which included a dozen or more family names drawn together through marriage and thus 'kinfolk.' The Hatfields lived in West Virginia and the McCoys in Kentucky. Bad blood between 'Devil Anse' Hatfield and Randall McCoy, the patriarchs of their respective clans, dated back to the Civil War but was quiescent until an argument developed over a razorback hog. While both clans were seething over the hog, Devil Anse's son, Jonse, complicated a difficult situation by taking up, as the mountain phrase had it, with Randall McCoy's daughter without the benefit of clergy. The explosion that followed brought the two states to the verge of Civil War.[1]

The above paragraph – with the author's permission – is taken from a fascinating book by John L. Spivak entitled, *A Man in His Time.* Chapter Six, "Incident at Matewan," explains in detail the background that led to Sid Hatfield's murder, as well as the virtual civil war then going on in West Virginia over the unionization of the coal mines. At the time, John Spivak was a young newspaper reporter who had been selected by the United Mine Workers as their emissary to Washington; there, he would plead with President Woodrow Wilson to put a stop to the labor conditions existing in West Virginia. As we know, Woodrow Wilson was bedfast and unable to function, but Mr. Spivak did see Presidential Assistant Joseph Tumulty, who was making virtually all major decisions. His interview with Tumulty is worth reading. Mr. Spivak's entire book is fascinating and provocative. He still writes, and lives not far from us in Riegelsville, Pennsylvania.

Sid Hatfield was accused of killing six of the Baldwin-Feltz Brothers

1. John L. Spivak, *A Man in His Time.* New York: Horizon Press, 1967, p. 88. Used by permission of the author.

– a detective agency hired by mine owners – and one of his assassins was a surviving Feltz brother. Mr. Spivak relates:

> About a year later, after I had left the coal fields and was working on a paper in New York, I read that Sid Hatfield had been arrested and charged with killing six of the Baldwin-Feltz men during the Matewan affair and had been ordered to appear for trial in Welch, West Virginia, a coal company town. With Sid were his wife and Ed Chambers, another descendant of the old Hatfield clan, and Ed's wife. At the urging of union officials who feared Hatfield would be assassinated by killers who would plead self-defense, Sid and Chambers left their guns at home, and it was publicly announced that they were going to Welch unarmed. As the two men and their wives walked up the courthouse steps on the morning of the trials, Lively, who had been leaning against a wall, turned to Hatfield with, 'Hello, Sid, glad to see you,' drew his pistol and started firing. Two notorious gunmen named George 'Buster' Penne and William Salters, who had also been leaning against a wall, drew their guns and emptied them on Hatfield and Chambers, who fell dead on the courthouse steps.[2]

One amusing incident developed from my witnessing this horrible murder. Two or three weeks later my firm asked me to come East for a meeting of the entire organization. Wanting to put in a good appearance, I purchased a new felt hat. In the hotel where the meeting was held I inadvertently placed my hat on a table near an ash tray containing a burning cigarette. The result was a hole in the brim of my new hat that looked exactly like a bullethole. Not being anxious to buy another hat, I kept wearing it. When my associates exclaimed, "Ike, what happened to your hat?" I replied with a straight face, "Did you read about Sid Hatfield's murder?" Everyone had. "Well, I was in my room in the hotel in Welch and went to my window to see what was happening, when one of the bullets ricocheted from the street, came through my window, and through my hat." I think most of them believed me.

2. *Ibid*, p. 92

CHAPTER THREE

LOGAN

Logan was the seat of some of the largest and most productive coal mines in West Virginia, most of them owned by the Island Creek Coal Company. Situated about sixty or seventy miles from Huntington, its only access was by a branch line of the C.&O. Railroad. Despite the short distance, it was a three-hour ride because of steep grades and numerous stops. As usual, the train left Huntington at 6:00 a.m. Someone had told me that there was great wealth there; I never needed much encouragement, so before long I found myself aboard this all day coach bound for Logan.

Arriving about 9:00 a.m., I registered at the only hotel, and washed off some coal black (train windows were always open) before my first call on the bank. As I have said, the banks were prospective clients and if the bank president was of good will, he would frequently reveal the names of men in town who might be prospective clients. This is what happened in Logan, where the bank president sent me to see three people, one of them being the famous sheriff, Don Chafin.

John Spivak tells quite a story in *A Man in His Time* about Logan, and speaks of Don Chafin. The following article, released by Associated Press at the time of Chafin's death, reveals some facts about this remarkable man:

DON CHAFIN, A LEADER IN THE COAL WARS OF WEST VIRGINIA IN 1920-21, DIES AT 67

Aug. 9 (AP)—Don Chafin, former sheriff of Logan County, W. Va., who led a force in battle against armed union men in the southern West Virginia mines wars of 1920-21, died today in Memorial Hospital. Mr. Chafin, who was 67 years old, succumbed of a heart attack following an operation.

The marching song of the union miners during those years was "Hang Don Chafin to a Sour Apple Tree." They never did. Mr. Chafin was one of the objectives of the "armed march" of 1921. He mustered a force of several thousand along the ridges at the border of the county to oppose the advance of union miners and their sympathizers from the coal fields in counties farther north. The northern forces were determined to organize the Logan County coal fields.

Mr. Chafin's men were given militia status by the Governor. They blocked the advance of the union men who never got past the ridges of Blair Mountain on the Boone-Logan County border. Thousands of shots were fired, but the casualties were few.

The Logan sheriff was a prominent figure in a series of trials in which union miners and union officials were charged with causing the deaths of three deputies in a skirmish when the two forces first faced each other. Eventually all cases except three in which convictions had been obtained, were dropped.

A few years later Mr. Chafin faced trial in a liquor conspiracy case. He served part of a two-year term, then went back to Logan on parole and resumed his place as a leading citizen.

He was one of Huntington's wealthiest men. His holdings included coal, oil and gas lands in Logan County, the Guaranty Bank Building, a building in downtown Logan and a large farm in Athalia, Ohio.

Mr. Chafin lived in a penthouse here on top of the ten-story Guaranty Building, which he had bought for $100,000. He also maintained another home in Hollywood, Fla.

His widow resides in Miami, Fla., with a daughter, Miss Lily Hazel Chafin, one of eight surviving children.

I called on Chafin and we were soon on a first-name basis. He carried a big pistol on his hip, with notches cut in the handle accounting for the number of persons he had killed. Whether one admired him or not he was a great personality, and was very helpful to me in Logan.

I was unfortunate enough to be in Logan the day of the armed march described in the above article. It was a holocaust. Miners' families were frightened and hysterical. Women and children, old men and women, fled from town on foot, with a few belongings hurriedly thrown over their shoulders. The railroad was their only means of exodus, but many fled into the woods or hid in their cellars.

I took refuge in the hotel, a fairly substantial brick building, and waited until the shooting was over. I could not get the regular four o'clock train (it didn't run), so I spent the night in Logan. I often think of this day as "a day to remember."

CHAPTER FOUR

PITTSBURGH TO WASHINGTON

Early in 1924 I was asked to move from West Virginia to the Pittsburgh office. My firm asked if I could hold my West Virginia business from Pittsburgh and I assured them I could. In this business a highly personalized relationship assures one of continuity, providing he is doing a good job – so we decided to move to Pittsburgh.

We elected to send our furniture by steamboat up the Ohio River; rates were much less than by rail. That year we were plagued by a severe drought and the river was unusually low. The boat carrying our furniture ran aground on an island near Gallipolis. It was two months before they could dislodge it, so we were compelled to rent a furnished apartment. When our furniture finally arrived it was so dried out that many pieces readily fell apart, requiring quite a rebuilding job.

During 1924 I was very busy getting the Pittsburgh office established. It was an especially eventful year for us because our only daughter, Elaine, was born.

In 1924 Calvin Coolidge had been in the White House for two years and was reelected for four remaining years. I believe most people will agree that he was a colorless and most conservative man. He espoused a policy of laissez-faire. But the nation took things into its hands. We had recovered fully from World War I and while money rates were high, business began to boom. Speculation in stocks and real estate had started and it continued at a dizzy pace until we reached the collapse of October, 1929. Stocks could be purchased on 10% margin and real estate for an even smaller margin. The collapse of the Florida land boom was as damaging in many respects as the collapse of the stock market. Why did not the authorities see this and put on the brakes? One has to believe that our administration was completely unaware of the dangers, or sound asleep.

In 1924 I was twenty-nine. I had been in the investment business for five years, but was still a neophyte. What policy did I follow with my clients? For two or three years I swam with the tide. One was almost forced to, and up until 1929, of course, the market kept rising.

From the very beginning I read everything that would be helpful in my business. My first love was *The Commercial and Financial Chronicle,* edited by Jacob Seibert and published by William B. Dana. It was a splendid publication, sound and conservative. In 1927 it started to warn people that there was entirely too much speculation and that we were headed for a crash. Of course they were ridiculed, but they stuck to their guns and I am sure thousands of people later regretted that they had not heeded the warnings.

Their logic somehow struck a chord with me. Maybe it was because I was so young, but fortunately I went along. Late in 1928 and through most of the first nine months of 1929, I advised my clients to gradually reduce holdings. For a while the market went against me, but I persisted. It wasn't easy to persuade people that this was the right course. Unless one has lived through a speculative era such as 1925–1929, it is difficult to realize what a frenzy prevailed. Some of my West Virginia clients had purchased real estate in Florida and within four or five years experienced fantastic appreciation. But in the end many of them lost all they had invested, and this was equally true in the stock market.

In the meantime, though, the Pittsburgh office flourished. I continued to go to West Virginia once a month, but early in 1929 my firm asked me to go to Washington and manage the office there. We were thrilled at the thought of living in Washington. One had to concede that Pittsburgh at that time was a dirty city. I went ahead and lived at the Racquet Club for two months while Helen remained in Pittsburgh to sell our house. We purchased a house on Primrose Street in beautiful Chevy Chase. Harland Jr. had been born in 1926 and now Dick was on his way.

Living in Washington during this period was a delightful experience which we thoroughly enjoyed. Schools were good and within walking distance.

The crash came in October of that year and regardless of where one lived it produced grave problems. My own family was affected very little; my salary remained the same, and I had sold what few stocks we owned. But chaos prevailed throughout the nation.

It was amazing to find that people in all walks of life had been playing the market – doctors, lawyers, chauffeurs, bootblacks and farmers – and most on a 10% margin. But stock prices did not reflect real values; they represented the hunches and guesses of speculators who hoped that in a few days other speculators would buy at still higher prices. From 1927 to 1929, except for occasional reactions, the figures rose in a dizzy spiral. Everyone expected to get rich.

On September 3, 1929, prices on New York Stock Exchange hit an all-time high. Stocks reached pinnacles that were incredible and ridiculous.

A few examples:*

American Telephone	$300
New York Central Railroad	$250
United States Steel	$250
Radio Corporation of America	$500
General Electric	$396

*Unadjusted for subsequent splits.

The well-known Dow-Jones Industrial Average rested on an all-time high of 381.17 on September 3. From this pinnacle prices were to plummet in six short weeks to 198.69. No stocks would be spared in the deluge.

CHAPTER FIVE

MARCHING TO BEDLAM

National City Bank encouraged its employees to invest in its shares and actually loaned them money to make their purchases. The stock sold between 488 and 802 in 1927, and in 1929 reached the fantastic price of 1400. I had a close friend in the bank, a senior officer who pyramided and bought to the hilt. When the crash came he owed the bank a large sum of money and the bank agreed to deduct a portion of his salary each month until the loan was liquidated. For several years he lived very frugally, and I am not sure that when he died fifteen years later all of the debt had been paid.

The Goldman Sachs Trading Corporation, an investment trust, was offered in 1928 at 104 per share. Its price subsequently soared to 326, and then tumbled in the crash to $1.75 – wiping out hundreds of investors in the process.

The plunge in radio stocks was equally damaging. Crosley Radio, selling at 63 times earnings, dropped from a high of 127 early in the year to 15 in October of 1929. It later declined to $2.50.

Grigsby Grunow, selling at 92 times earnings at its peak of 80, declined to 14 and later, in 1932, to 75 cents. Raytheon sold at a high of 81 and declined to 18 in the early break – later to 50 cents a share. The list goes on and on.

Various things contributed to the debacle culminating in October 1929. A few were:

1. Negligence on the part of the administration and the Federal Reserve banks;
2. The lack of restrictive governmental agencies such as the SEC (formed in 1934);
3. Over-speculation in Florida real estate;
4. Inflation and troublesome times in Europe;
5. Low margin requirements.

To illustrate what carelessness was shown by many of our leading banks and investment bankers, millions and millions of dollars' worth of foreign bonds were sold to American investors in the late Twenties; and a large percentage of these defaulted within a short space of time. Looking back, it seems incredible that our leading bankers could have been so short-sighted and avaricious. Below are listed a few of the issues offered. In many cases investors lost all principal and collected very little interest.

1. $27,000,000 Government of Argentina 6%'s due 1961;
2. $10,000,000 State of Rio Grande do Sul (Brazil) 7%'s due 1966;
3. $6,500,000 Province of Mendoza (Argentina) 7-½'s due 1951;
4. $5,000,000 Dominican Republic 5-½'s due 1940;
5. $3,000,000 Municipality of Medellin (Colombia) 7%'s due 1951;
6. $6,000,000 Lombard Electric Co. (Italy) 7%'s due 1952;
7. $30,000,000 City of Rome 6-½'s due 1952;
8. $15,000,000 Republic of Peru 7%'s due 1959;
9. $7,000,000 Bank of East Prussia Landowners Assn. 6%'s due 1929;
10. $6,000,000 State of Pernambuco (Brazil) 7%'s due 1947.

These represent only a few of the large number of foreign bonds sold – as sound investments – to a gullible and unsuspecting public, who realized too late the inferior quality of the issues. There is nothing to be gained by naming the underwriters here, but they represented the best-known and most highly respected names in the investment banking industry.

IVAR KREUGER

The financing done by the above gentleman – along with the sale of all the foreign bonds – illustrates further how very naive and gullible were our American bankers.

This famous "Match King" was undoubtedly one of the greatest of all international crooks. Handsome, debonair, smooth, he could virtually charm a bird out of a tree. In 1913 he began to form a Match Trust to control factories, forests and mines in Europe. It eventually became a huge international finance agency. After obtaining all the money he could from European investors, he came to the United States, and between 1925 and 1929 he milked investors of millions and millions of dollars. And he did it so smoothly that few realized what was going on until it was all over.

Impeccably dressed and with manners that were suave and sophisticated, he started his machinations through one of the best-known investment banking firms in America, headquartered in Boston. He falsified statements, exaggerated his assets and did everything that was misleading and dishonest. But somehow American bankers and American investment bankers took him at his word and swallowed his story, hook, line and sinker. After his introduction to Boston bankers and investment firms, Kreuger went to New York and there was accorded an even greater welcome than the one he received in Boston. From this point on, he attracted bankers and investment firms as molasses attracts flies. He didn't have to go any further. Men from the Middle West and the West came to him.

At first only the common stock of his fabulous firm, Kreuger & Toll, was offered. The amount available was inexhaustible. Finally, he started to offer his bonds, and for three or four years investors absorbed both with great enthusiasm. And why not? Weren't they being recommended by the best-known names – banks as well as investment bankers – in America?

Eventually the collapse came, and although some of the bond principal was recovered, most of the money went down the drain. Ivar Kreuger committed suicide and American investors, who were duped, had no recourse. We were then without the SEC, or any laws that offered protection to the investor.

From *The Commercial and Financial Chronicle,* warnings began as early as 1926:

"In the closing month of 1926 there were no new or startling developments, either here or abroad. Indications of a moderate recession in certain lines of domestic trade, from the extreme activity reached in the autumn, persisted. This was particularly true in the case of the steel trade and the automobile industry, but seemed nevertheless a situation that might have to be reckoned with as affecting probable industrial conditions in the immediate future; this was the more so in view of the great decline in the price of cotton, as the result of the huge crop produced in 1926, which served to impair the purchasing capacity of an important section of the country, and in view also of the fact that the agricultural classes of the west are likewise far from being over-prosperous. On the other hand, comfort was derived from the character of President Coolidge's message to Congress and from the action of the United States Steel Corporation in recommending the declaration of a 4% stock dividend to represent the surplus income accumulated through the quarter century of the existence of this, the foremost industrial corporation of the world. It was reasoned that the directors of this company, always so conservatively managed, would not have taken such a step at the present time, did they not regard the immediate future of the country's industries and of the steel trade in particular with the utmost confidence and assurance."

January, 1927:

"As in previous months, the high-priced shares were particularly prominent in fluctuation, and their movements up and down most of the time controlled the course of the general market. Among the railroad stocks Atchison common was pre-eminently the leader. With earnings far in excess of the dividends paid, talk was indulged in with growing frequency of the probability of a stock dividend like that made by the Steel Corporation. After the close of the year the Atchison announced merely ¾ of 1% extra, in addition to the regular quarterly payment of 1 ¾%. The stock sold up from 153 1/8 December 1 to 172 December 24, and closed December 31 at 170 3/8. Among other railroads, Central New Jersey rose from 283 December 8 to 295 1/4 December 17, and closed December 31 at 290; Lehigh Valley ($50 shares) from 92 7/8 December 1 to 106 December 10, with the close December 31 100; Union Pacific common from 159 3/8 December 6 to 165 3/4 December 20, with the close December 31 162 1/4. Southern Railway advanced from 116 1/4 December 3 to 126 3/4 December 31."

From these quotations one can see that there was considerable speculation as early as December, 1926. Continuing, *The Chronicle* states:

"Great activity developed on the Stock Exchange during February [1927] and notable advances in prices occurred nearly all through the list of stocks, many of the upward spurts being of spectacular proportions. The tone most of the time was positively buoyant and the volume of transactions exceeded that of any previous February in the history of the Exchange, with next to the heaviest day's business on the last day, February 28, on which day the strength of the market was perhaps most pronounced of all. Aggregate transactions in stocks during the month reached 44,162,496 shares, as compared with 35,725,989 shares in February 1926, 32,794,456 shares in 1925 and 20,721,562 shares in 1924. After February 3 the business exceeded 2,000,000 shares a day on every day except one (barring the Saturday half holidays), while on at least two days the business got close to 3,000,000 shares, the transactions on February 8 reaching 2,845,060 shares and those on February 28 2,543,290 shares. Early in the month the railroad stocks were the dominating features, both high-priced and low-priced issues being rushed up with great rapidity, but later in the month when it appeared that the reaction in general trade, which had been under way for some time, had about reached its end and was now giving place to slow recovery, the industrial shares were brought to the front and whirled upward with even greater speed than the rails, while the specialties indulged in the performances always witnessed on such occasions."

In October of 1927, *The Chronicle* observes:

"During the past year we have had few general reactions in the stock market which partook of the nature of the reaction of February and March 1926, or even that of October 1926. Probably the principal reason for this has been the discrimination in the selection of stocks, the selling of those which were relatively high, and the purchase of those which seemed relatively low. And yet, admitting all this, the general level of prices is now so high that it must be considered as discounting in a most liberal, nay extravagant, fashion, everything of a favorable nature that may happen, while leaving entirely out of the account anything of an unfavorable nature, such as trade reaction, with which the country is now laboring, and falling railroad earnings, which are now also an unfortunate feature of affairs."

Early in December, 1927:

"The stock market the present week has shown considerable irregularity, and at times decided weakness. Activity has been maintained at a high level, and with money and credit easy, it has not been difficult to advance with great rapidity special stocks and special groups of stocks. Indeed, that has been the chief characteristic of the market of late, namely, that the specialties have commanded most attention. Every day half a dozen or more of these are taken in hand and whirled up with great rapidity. The more mystery and the more uncertainty there is as regards the merits of the stocks selected for manipulation the easier it is to find speculative support for them."

Later in December,

". . . Brokers' loans still keep moving merrily upward. The story this week is the same as in all other recent weeks, that is, another new high record in all time has been established. Nor is the further addition the present week small, especially considering the extent of the previous additions and the fact that it is piled on top of a total itself of unparalleled magnitude. The week's increase is $51,956,000. With this further increase the grand total of the loans to brokers and dealers (secured by stocks and bonds) by the fifty-two reporting member banks of the Federal Reserve system in New York City is brought up to the huge figure of $3,562,805,000. This is the amount for Wednesday night, December 7. On December 8, 1926, when the amount was by no means small, the total was no more than $2,638,528,000. In other words, the increase for the twelve months is found to be $924,277,000, which affords an idea of the magnitude of the expansion that has taken place during this period of time. As heretofore, large increases are found in all the leading categories, the loans made by these reporting member banks for their own account now being $1,222,800,000, against $813,368,000 a year ago, an addition of fully 50%; the loans made for account of out-of-town banks $1,366,278,000, against $1,062,969,000, and the loans made for account of others $973,727,000 against $762,191,000."

In April, 1928:

"Two statements of brokers' loans have been made public the present week and both speak eloquently as to the extent to which the gigantic speculation on the Stock Exchange is being conducted on borrowed money. It is more than ordinarily important that the figures regarding these brokers' loans should be watched and pondered, inasmuch as the New York Clearing House last Saturday carried out its purpose to discontinue the Saturday weekly returns showing the loans and the reserve position of the Clearing House banks and trust companies which it had been the practice to give out during the whole three-quarters of a century since the organization of the Clearing House."

Two weeks later,

"All European markets showed intense interest in the speculative activity in New York. The opinion seemed to be general that the feverish activity here could not but be harmful in the long run 'The present condition in Wall Street,' a London dispatch of April 13 to *The*

New York Times said, 'is described as that of a patient in a high state of fever approaching a crisis, the only doubtful element being the degree of weakness which must follow its passing. That a severe reaction must ensue does not appear to admit of any doubt.' "

In September, 1928:

"The speculation for higher prices on the New York Stock Exchange made further progress the present week. Increasing buoyancy has been manifested and the upward movement has reached the proportions of a veritable boom."

And on December 29, 1928:

"There are a number of evils connected with the present frenzy of speculation that are collateral in nature and not associated with debt, money rates, or exchange seat prices. One of these is the unsettlement of stock prices. And by this we mean a permanent doubt cast upon the reality of present values. Those who preach prosperity in season and out, advising for instance 'never sell the United States short,' tend to create the idea that the 'bull market' will continue indefinitely, that there is a development, a growth, behind the boom that is a result of our expansion in exploitation of resources, advance in foreign trade, and increase in wealth. There is but a minimum of truth in this. For several years there has been little legitimate relation between the earning power of shares and their exchange price. No one can believe the high prices prevailing can continue for long. There must be a return eventually to the normal. And when this does come, what gauge will the investor have save earning power? And how will he be able to use this save in connection with market prices prevailing at the time? The 'bull' pressure will be a thing of the past. He cannot reasonably expect a new boom will immediately succeed. He may think he is buying in a depression. But though prices are low, will this new standard have any ascertainable relation to earning power?

"The result must be a permanent doubt thrown on all values. Thus the present boom is a detriment to future stability which will make itself apparent by a stagnation hard to overcome. And this notwithstanding there is a slow increase in values through natural expansion. Another effect closely associated with this will follow. There is an old saying, 'Seek money where it has been lost.' But a 'burnt child dreads the fire.' And a great city gains nothing in the so-called 'provinces' by absorbing the money of the country lost in speculation. Time was when 'Wall Street' stood for greed and corruption, chiefly through political anathema. But to be the home of bulls and bears who are devouring the savings of the people (only to devour themselves in turn) does not conduce to the confidence required for a sustained legitimate trade. And it is not too much to say that if this speculative orgy does not soon disappear there will be an undefined question asked of the great central banks themselves. This in turn would be a calamity to the whole country."

In January, 1929:

"Another week's return on brokers' loans by the Federal Reserve Bank of New York is at hand, and likewise another monthly statement by the New York Stock Exchange itself, and it is difficult for any well-informed commentator who has an appreciation of what figures of such magnitude as those contained therein mean – what a menace they involve to the entire community – to speak with restraint and in calm, temperate language, of the way the movement is proceeding, week after week and month after month, without the slightest indication that the end, the inevitable end, is in sight, or even near. It is impossible to characterize such a situation without resort to expressions and terms which to the ordinary mind will seem extreme; and yet the situation merits the severest strictures and really makes it a public duty for anyone in authority, or having influence and weight, to speak in unsparing terms in denunciation of what is going on! The pages of history would have to be scanned in vain to find anything quite parallel to it.

"Staid financiers, with a long record of experience in the financial world, look on in a dazed kind of way, evidently puzzled to know what to do about it, then complacently accept the situation on the theory that this is a big and growing country with vast and unlimited resources and therefore we must not be unduly disturbed by mere size – that borrowing for speculative purposes must be expected to be in proportion to everything else in this marvelous country of ours. But the way in which the movement is now progressing makes further dallying with it too grave a responsibility for any serious-minded person to face without a shudder."

June, 1929:

"The stock market during June completely reversed its course. After the very extensive break during May, it moved almost steadily upward in June and staged a broad recovery. Instead of the previous losses, advances now became the rule. While the declines suffered in May were by no means completely recovered, taking the Stock Exchange list as a whole, the market displayed growing strength almost from beginning to end of the month. In the case of special stocks, mostly of the high-priced type, the advances were really sensational by reason of their magnitude, and a whole host of share properties established new high records for the year. The leaders in the upward movement were the same as on previous occasions of buoyancy, being mainly gilt-edged properties of exceptional character and strength (though there were the usual few exceptions to the rule), and the confident buying of such shares – whether for investment or as a speculative move did not matter – gave tone to the entire market and eventually carried the whole list upward. If there was some hesitancy in renewing speculative efforts for a rise in the early part of the month after the sad experience during May, this hesitancy disappeared as the market swept upward all along the line. There appeared to be a disposition to view the money situation with growing complacency, and indeed during the first three weeks of the month the call loan rate on the Stock Exchange seemed stabilized at 7%, no change from that figure occurring even during the middle of the month when the United States Government was carrying through its customary large quarterly financing."

July, 1929:

"There is nothing to be said about the stock market the present week except that it has been strong to the point of buoyancy. Prices have been advancing by leaps and bounds, and the course has been steadily upward day after day, except that on Friday there was some downward reaction on very extensive sales to realize profits. The railroads are no longer an exception to the rule of higher prices, as was the case for so long, and with these also participating in the upward movement, the advance has been gaining great momentum. Dealings have become very broad in character, attesting the market's underlying strength. The money and the credit situation appear no longer to be giving traders any concern. The call loan rate on the Stock Exchange, which had been held firm all of last week at 10%, on Monday spurted to 15%, which was the rate also on Tuesday for all loans, including renewals. But this did not disturb the speculative fraternity in the least, and bullish proclivities kept growing stronger and still stronger." However, heavy liquidation had begun by the first of October, 1929:

"The only thing to be said about the stock market the week ending October 5 is that it has been continuously weak day after day, with heavy declines in prices, and with only fitful rallies now and then. The call loan rate touched 10% on both Monday and Tuesday, which, of course, did not tend to improve sentiment, but the market still remained weak on Wednesday, when the call loan rate in the afternoon fell to 7%, and was weakest of all on Thursday, when the rate dropped to 6% after renewals had been effected at 7 ½%. On this last mentioned day a new depressing influence was the Stock Exchange statement of brokers' loans, showing a further increase of $667,764,553, on top of increases of $400,000,000 a month in each of the three preceding months, and bringing the grand total of Stock Exchange borrowings up to over 8 ½ billion dollars – in exact figures, $8,549,383,979. On Friday the call loan rate again touched 6% without benefit to the market. It was impossible to stop the avalanche of selling, and the further increase in brokers' loans of $43,000,000 shown in the weekly statement of the New York Reserve Bank for the week ending Wednesday proved additionally disturbing. There was an upward reaction the middle of the day, but renewed weakness in the closing hour. Liquidation all through the week was on an extensive scale and yesterday it was perfectly overwhelming, with all support lacking, though brokers claim that they had extensive buy orders to fill for their customers as prices moved down – orders given some time ago, in expectation of just such a break as has actually occurred."

On Wednesday, October 23, the market roared toward "Black Thursday" and its October 29 climax. Mother Nature can be cruel in many ways. The morning of the twenty-third dawned clear and lovely in New York, but the midwest was swept by an unseasonably early and heavy snowstorm. The decline in the market began at the opening bell on the Floor of the Exchange, but the storm in the west brought down telephone and telegraph wires, hampering all lines of communication. This only added fuel to the fire and signs of panic multiplied. The day's trading of over 6,000,000 shares was the second largest in history; reports of sales and purchases were as much as seven hours late.

Naturally, margin calls by the thousands went out that night, and the whole nation was in a state of gloom. But few realized on the night of the twenty-third that the next day would bring trading volume of twice the day before, going down in history as "Black Thursday."

On October 24 the selling began quietly enough, but gathered momentum and volume as the morning progressed. By 11:30 panic had taken over on the Floor. Everyone wanted to liquidate, and buyers had disappeared. Ticker tapes across the country were running late with their tabulations of collapsing quotations and prices, and a crowd had gathered outside the Exchange building. Conditions were so frenzied that visitors were denied entrance, including Sir Winston Churchill.

But even as visitors were being ushered from the Exchange, a temporary respite was being brought to the Floor. At noon the news spread that a meeting of important bankers was taking place at J. P. Morgan's office, including Charles Mitchell of National City Bank, William C. Potter from Guaranty Trust Co., Albert H. Wiggins, Chase National Bank, and Seward Prosser of Bankers Trust Co. Bernard Baruch had been invited to join the group, but had declined. These gentlemen thought the time had come to organize support for the market, and were willing to put up forty million dollars to buy stocks – hopefully putting an end to the frenzied liquidations. They were correct temporarily. Richard Whitney appeared and offered to buy U. S. Steel at 205, although the last sale had been at 195. Immediately fear disappeared and prices were much firmer. But the rally did not last long, and prices were soon sinking lower and faster.

"Black Thursday was only the overture. The ticker, unable to keep up with the rapidity of transactions, ran until seven o'clock that evening before completing the recording of trades .... The next day President Hoover said, 'The fundamental business of the country .... is on a sound and prosperous basis.' There was a two-day rally on Friday and Saturday, but on Monday the decline resumed and on Tuesday the 29th, the holocaust went far beyond the possibility of control and the national depression was on."[3]

The November 2 issue of *The Commercial and Financial Chronicle* went on to comment vividly upon the week's frenzied activities: "The current week is one that will long be remembered in the annals of the New York Stock Exchange. The huge declines of the previous week and the worldwide publicity given to the record breaking sales on the preceding Thursday, culminated on Tuesday in the most frenzied liquidation the Exchange has ever experienced. The turnover broke all previous records and at the close had reached the unprecedented total of 16,410,030 shares. Recessions were recorded in practically every active stock, and ranged from a dozen points to 45 or more. As the week advanced prices improved but the avalanche of sales was so great that the Board of Governors of the New York Stock Exchange voted on Wednesday to defer the opening of the Exchange until 12 o'clock on

3. John Brooks, *Once in Golconda.* New York: Harper & Row, Publishers, p. 118. Used by permission.

Thursday, and keep the Exchange closed altogether on Friday and Saturday. This would suspend further sessions until Monday, November 4, in order to save Wall St. employees from breakdown."

This was, indeed, a week long to be remembered in the annals of the New York Stock Exchange. It ushered in a Depression and a decade fraught with economic and social difficulties more profound than any our nation had faced to date.

SOLD OUT

October 25, 1929

PART TWO

1930-1940

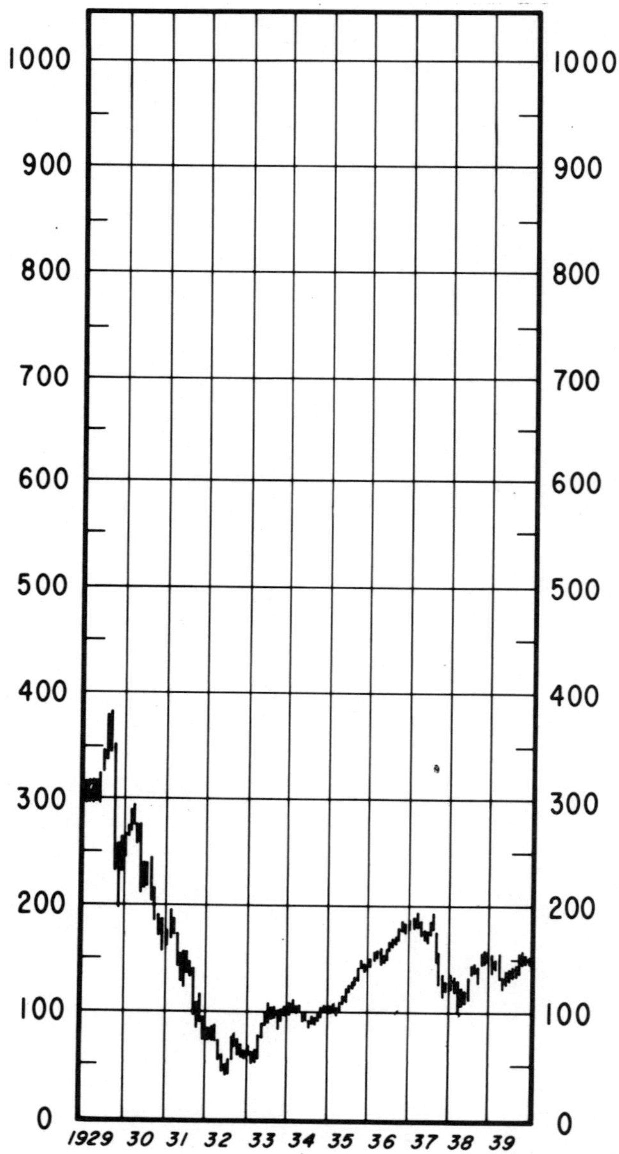
1000
900
800
700
600
500
400
300
200
100
0
1929 30 31 32 33 34 35 36 37 38 39

CHAPTER ONE

"BROTHER, CAN YOU SPARE A DIME?"

1930 and 1931 were difficult years. We did well to hold our old accounts, because new ones were just not available. Most people were too frightened to make investments even if they had the funds. We managed to keep our heads above water, but, late in 1931, I received a real blow when my firm asked me to return to Pittsburgh. The office there was not doing well and it was felt that I could put new life into it. At first I declined, but in the end a good salary increase persuaded me to accept.

We left Washington with our four children on January 1, 1932. The Depression had struck cruelly in industrial cities such as Pittsburgh, Cleveland, Detroit and Chicago. The contrast between Pittsburgh and Washington was striking. Half of the store windows on Wood Street, where most of the well-known shops were located, were boarded over. Unemployment was widespread. Breadlines and souplines prevailed everywhere. Men who in the recent past had been successful salesmen or productive in many walks of life stood on street corners selling apples and shoe strings.

We rented an apartment in a nice section of the East End, across the street from Andrew Mellon's beautiful estate, and we had a constant stream of people at our door begging for food. Eggs could be purchased for ten cents a dozen, hamburger for fifteen cents a pound. Help could be had for a dollar a day. We had a sweet Scottish woman who worked for us by the week, and frequently we paid her wages a week or two in advance so that the utility companies would not shut off her gas and electricity.

"And as despair settled like a dark pall over workers in and from the cities, so, too, during 1930 and 1931, it deepened among the nation's farmers. The Wall Street Crash had worsened the plight of farmers who had already been through a decade of diminishing income. Farm prices fell 30 per cent during the first two years of the Depression. Corn sold for 15 cents a bushel, cotton and wool went for 5 cents a pound, hogs brought 3 cents, and beef 2.5 cents a pound. And farmers didn't know what to do about it – except keep production up, or actually increase it, thereby adding to the slide in prices. Industry could always cut back production to maintain prices, but in 1929 and 1930 farmers feared to cut back production; it required every scrap of produce they could raise just to keep them going at those prices. Farm income, nationwide, fell by 33 per cent from 1929 to 1931 . . . ."[1]

Unless one lived through this period, it is difficult to realize how real the suffering and misery were. To say that it was all depressing would be putting it mildly. The nation was enveloped with gloom.

As we approached the 1932 Presidential election, when Franklin Delano Roosevelt would be nominated by the Democratic Party to oppose Herbert Hoover, the nation was in deep trouble. Hoover in many respects was a great man and a sincere humanitarian, but he had not grasped in time the seriousness of the crises that faced the nation, nor taken steps to halt the wild speculation in the stock market that contributed to its steep decline.

The Crash of October and November, 1929, ushered in an economic depression which continued throughout Hoover's administration. As counter-measures Hoover did recommend an extensive public works program and conducted a vigorous campaign against what he called "unjustified fear." He appointed several commissions, such as the National Commission on Law Observance and Law Enforcement, to study the various problems confronting the administration. He extended relief to the victims of the great drought of 1930, and countless farmers were aided by the Federal Farm Board. The Reconstruction Finance Corporation which Hoover created stimulated industry, making loans that could not be obtained through normal channels. And he established the Emergency Relief Act and the Federal Home Loan Bank.

Conditions abroad were troublesome, particularly in Germany and Japan, and Hoover attempted to assist these two powers. But the apathy and gloom which pervaded domestic and foreign prospects deepened, and Hoover received little credit for many constructive moves that he initiated.

Up to 1928 it would seem that Hoover's career had been a complete success. Born in West Branch, Iowa, of Quaker parents, ambitious and studious, he graduated from Stanford University with honors. He became a mining engineer with a British mining company in China and had made a large fortune when still a young man. After organizing

---

1. Robert Goldston, *The Great Depression*. Indianapolis: The Bobbs-Merrill Co., Inc., 1968, pp. 51-52. Used by permission.

famine relief in Belgium, Hoover was made Secretary of Commerce in Harding's administration and continued under Coolidge. He was easily elected President in 1928. But events soon proved that he was not equipped to cope with the problems that were to face him.

> What the country needs is a good, big laugh. There seems to be a condition of hysteria. If someone could get off a good joke every ten days, I think our troubles would be over.
>
> –Herbert Hoover

Hoover displayed a rather cold, austere attitude. His questionable judgment was best demonstrated during the veterans' march on Washington in 1932. Millions of veterans were out of work and felt that the government should assist them. They received little sympathy and finally decided on the march. Most of them were peace-loving, respectable citizens, and they converged on Washington, living in paper shanties and shacks. Instead of the looked-for sympathy, they received tear gas and bayonet jabs as they were run out of the Capitol. Had it not been for Pelham D. Glassford, Superintendent of Washington Police, a bloody incident might have occurred. When the veterans standing outside the Capitol Building heard that the Senate had vetoed a bonus bill, they were about to charge into the building. Glassford talked them out of any display, and persuaded them to join in singing "America" prior to disbursing.

In 1924, World War I veterans had received adjusted compensation certificates entitling them to a payment averaging $1000 each to be made in 1945. In 1936, Congress finally passed a law permitting them to exchange their certificates for cashable bonds. Following this, most individual states voted veterans' bonuses in varying amounts. But the famous March on Washington in 1932 and the harsh treatment received from the administration undoubtedly hastened such action.

CHAPTER TWO

THE LONG ROAD BACK

"The year 1932 opened with a sense of crisis in the air. Now the unemployment figure had reached 14 million, and was still rising rapidly. National income had declined by 50 per cent (from $87.5 billion to $41.7 billion) since those remote and faintly incredible days of 1929. Manufacturing had declined by more than 50 per cent; the American economy was grinding to a standstill. And those who still retained jobs were earning, for example, 5 cents an hour in saw mills, and $2.39 for a fifty-hour work week in textile mills; children in Connecticut were earning 75 cents a week for fifty-five hours of hard work in certain sweatshops. Now the breadlines included former shopkeepers, former businessmen, former middle-class housewives. But local relief agencies could no longer support the burden; by 1932 only one quarter of America's unemployed were actually receiving help."[2]

By the time Roosevelt was inaugurated in March, 1933, the Depression had become deep-seated. Millions of men were out of work, beggars walked the streets, and a general pall enveloped the nation. Probably the one event that accentuated the seriousness of our situation more than any other was the declaration of a Bank Holiday on March 6, 1933, when every bank in the nation was closed by the order of the President. Prior to the closings, depositors had been withdrawing their money and placing it in safe deposit boxes, or taking it home.

The President's action was hastened somewhat by the State of Michigan. On February 14, 1933, the Governor of Michigan had been compelled to declare a bank holiday. Michigan was highly industrialized and felt the Depression more severely, perhaps, than any other state. This action helped to precipitate the nationwide Holiday declared by President Roosevelt on March 6.

On March 10, by Executive Order, the President authorized the Secretary of the Treasury and the appropriate supervisory authority in each state to permit the reopening of banks on the condition that state nonmember banks obtain a license from a state authority and member

2. *Ibid*, p. 57

banks obtain a license from the Secretary of the Treasury. (Member banks belonged by membership to the Federal Reserve Banking System; nonmembers did not.) Procedurally, a license application from the Treasury was filed with the Federal Reserve Bank, and, upon approval by the Secretary of the Treasury, was issued by the Federal Reserve Bank. Such approval was based upon recommendations from the Comptroller of the Currency for national banks and the district Federal Reserve Bank for state member banks.

On March 11, the following schedule was announced by the President for the reopening of the country's commercial banks:

March 13: Banks in the twelve Federal Reserve cities that had been closed seven days;

March 14: Banks in the 250 cities with clearing houses that had been closed eight days;

March 15: All other licensed member banks that had been closed nine days.

The banks were relegated into four groups. Those considered fully sound, with assets equal to their deposits, were allowed to resume unrestricted payments. Under the March 11 schedule, fifty percent of the banking resources were opened by March 15. Twenty-five percent of the nation's banks, considered in less sound condition, were permitted to pay out a percentage of their deposits. The third group was placed in the hands of conservators. And, finally, five percent of the nation's banks, numbering about 1000, were closed permanently.

The straight licensing program took about a month, and by April 12, 1933, it was completed. At that time, 4789 national banks, 636 state member banks, and 7392 nonmember banks – a total of 12,817 – were open for business. Of the 4067 which failed to reopen by April 12, 1108 were national banks, and 2959 were nonmember banks.

In general, however, few banks that were opened before April 12 were subsequently reorganized; after that date most of them were. Under this licensing system, 1905 remained unlicensed on December 30, 1933 – 452 national banks, sixty state member banks and 1393 nonmember banks.

The Illinois Banking system in particular is of interest during these difficult years. The great majority of banks in Illinois were small, even in Chicago. Of 224 banks operating in Chicago in 1929, only eleven had assets of more than $10 million. In the rest of the six county metropolitan areas, only one of 221 banks had assets of more than $10 million.

In the years following the stock market crash, a large part of the banking facilities of Chicago and Illinois disappeared. In four years, more than three-fourths of the banks in Chicago vanished as a result of failures, absorptions, mergers, and closings, declining from 224 operating banks at the end of 1929 to fifty-four at the end of 1933. In Illinois as a whole, about half of the banking offices disappeared in four years – from 1,765 banks at the end of 1929 to 875 at the end of 1933.

By the end of 1939, Chicago still had only fifty-four operating banks compared with 224 in 1929. Reduction in the number of small banks was most severe. As of 1939, there were only twenty-eight operating banks in Chicago with assets of less than $10 million compared with 183 in the previous decade.

The decline in banking facilities subsequent to 1929 was relatively greater in Chicago than in other leading cities studied. In 1929, Chicago had been similar to other leading unit banking centers (St. Louis, Dallas, Denver) in number of commercial bank offices relative to the population, but lost so large a proportion of its bank facilities that in 1939 only sixteen bank offices per million were in operation, with recovery to nineteen by 1949 and twenty-two by 1959. As of 1959, it had only two-thirds as many bank offices relative to its population as other leading unit-bank cities, and only one-fourth as many as the average of the twelve leading multiple office bank cities in the nation.

J. M. (100%) NICHOLS

One of the most intriguing stories concerning Chicago banks during the Bank Holiday and the period following was that of J. M. Nichols, who was President of the First National Bank of Englewood, a Chicago suburb. An arch conservative and a banker's banker, this gentleman demonstrated not only that sound and conservative banking practices kept his own bank in perfect condition, but also that most of our banking troubles – including the Bank Holiday – could have been avoided had his policies and practices been followed by the banking fraternity.

A fascinating book could be written about Mr. Nichols. So liquid was his bank at the time of the Bank Holiday that he was dubbed "100% Nichols." Hale and hearty at eighty-nine, he still resides in suburban Hinsdale.

J. M. Nichols displayed the courage of refusing to join the deposit plan sponsored by the federal government, and threatened to close his bank if the U. S. got too tough. He called the plan a farce – and finally won his fight. Later he announced plans to remove his cash from the Federal Reserve Bank, sarcastically placing a value of ten cents per share on the Reserve Bank's stock. On September 14, 1935, he finally agreed to join the Federal Deposit Insurance Corporation, but on October 19, 1938, renewed his war with the FDIC and refused to supply deposit data. Finally, in 1941, he closed his bank voluntarily. Depositors were paid in full, and the stockholders also fared very well.

The following excerpts from *The Chicago Tribune* chronicle these unique events in the life of a gentleman banker who was himself unique in this or any other period.

NICHOLS REFUSES TO JOIN IN BANKS' INTEREST BOOST

J. M. Nichols, Englewood banker, yesterday took issue with the Chicago Clearing House association with respect to the interest rate to be paid on demand deposits. In a letter to depositors of the First National Bank of Englewood, of which he is president, Mr. Nichols stated:

"We are not increasing the rate of interest paid on demand deposits to 1 per cent, as is being done by the Chicago Clearing House association. This is an unbusiness-like piece of window dressing, coming, as it does, at a time when practically every bank in Chicago is passing dividends, cutting salaries, or losing money.

"Our present rate of one-fourth of 1 per cent must stand on those demand accounts whose average monthly balances exceed $3,000. You must rest assured that we will raise the rate at such time as we deem it in keeping with common sense and sound banking."

—March 29, 1933

DEPOSITORS HEED NICHOLS' CALL TO COME AND GET IT

100% Banker Returns Savings Funds.

Holders of savings accounts in the First National Bank of Englewood have nearly completed the withdrawal of their funds at the request of the bank, J. M. Nichols, president, reported yesterday. He said that only about $48,000, involving accounts awaiting settlement of inheritance taxes, remains in the savings department.

The banker, known as "100 per cent Nichols" because his bank for years has maintained liquid assets more than sufficient to pay off all depositors, first asked patrons to withdraw their savings accounts in a letter mailed April 23.

Owners Best Custodians.

Again, on May 7, he warned customers to call for their savings fund, saying in part: "The time is here when I believe you can best act as the custodian of your own funds."

Nichols' bank has not paid any interest on savings deposits since last December. Instead, it has been making a small charge to cover the cost of insuring the deposits with the Federal Deposit Insurance Corporation.

Peak Above 4 Millions.

The bank had $2,018,000 of savings accounts on Jan. 2, 1941. In the early 1930s they had reached a high mark of $4,685,000.

Yesterday Nichols said concerning the decision to drop savings deposits:

"From our point of view there is no chance of investing the money in the way we would like, safely and profitably, and we felt it was our duty to hand it back to the owners."

—June 4, 1941

CHAPTER THREE

THE NEW DEAL

Franklin D. Roosevelt promised the nation "A New Deal" during his campaign for the Presidency. Throughout his thirteen years in the White House, his administration was identified with this phrase, and it still is.

In his first one hundred days, Franklin Roosevelt led a floundering society back to self-confidence, and no President since 1933 has been allowed to forget it. John F. Kennedy complained shortly before assuming power, "I am sick of hearing about a hundred days. I am not a Roosevelt, and these aren't the Thirties."

"The President carried with him so many Democratic Congressmen that it was found impossible to seat all seventy-five Democratic Senators on the Democratic side of the aisle in the Senate; twelve had to sit with the Republicans. The Republican Party seemed doomed. Someone hung a large banner across the highway leading from New Hampshire into Maine which read, 'You Are Now Leaving the United States.' *The New York Times* observed that so great was FDR's influence that 'If he were to say a kind word about the man-eating shark, people would look thoughtful and say perhaps there are two sides to the question.'

"There was no doubt that the New Deal was overwhelmingly popular with the American people. But this was not simply because of the Roosevelt charm, nor was it simply because of the success of New Deal measures. Many were unsuccessful; the Depression had not been licked. But the people felt that there was someone in the White House who was, basically, on their side. And in 1936, at least, that was sufficient."[3]

As Franklin Roosevelt took over the reins of the nation, we had just ended the first third of the twentieth century, which had seen America emerge from her political isolation. The second third was to hand us the leadership of the Western world.

In the first thirty-three years, we experienced the introduction of the telephone, the automobile, and the airplane, as well as the First

3. *Ibid*, p. 151

World War, the Soviet Revolution and the worst economic depression in history. Perhaps it was well that we didn't realize or could foresee that the second third of the century was to bring even greater upheavals – the Second World War, atomic power, intercontinental rockets, the Korean War, Vietnam, the Chinese Revolution, television, NASA, satellites, moonlandings, and one of the greatest bull markets in stock market history.

So many constructive things happened in 1933 that the nation began to feel better. The Federal Deposit Insurance Corporation did much to restore people's confidence in banks following the Holiday. In rapid succession we then had the Agricultural Adjustment Act, the National Recovery Act, Works Progress Administration, Public Works Administration; and the Reconstruction Finance Corporation was made more effective.

Perhaps what lifted spirits most was the annulment of Prohibition. The Volstead Act, forbidding the manufacture or sale of alcoholic beverages, had been passed just after World War I, over Woodrow Wilson's veto. This innocuous and inane legislation, sponsored by Congressman Andrew J. Volstead of Minnesota, created gangsterism, bootlegging and powerful racketeers such as Chicago's Al Capone and his gang, who defied the law only to become millionaires.

During Prohibition, New York City's 15,000 saloons were replaced by 32,000 speakeasies, and the bootlegger became something of a public benefactor. Profits from illicit liquor corrupted the police and the judiciary.

During Prohibition, drugstores had been permitted to carry whiskey for medicinal purposes. Ailments abounded. With the repeal of the Amendment, early in 1933, druggists were ordered to dispose of all their inventory within sixty days. Our druggist in Pittsburgh was located about five blocks away from our apartment, and was suddenly swamped by people who wished to get a supply of whiskey. I got to his store as soon as I could. He had only two cases of choice bourbon left, which he sold to me for $2.00 per quart. What a bargain! Happy days were here again.

Robert Goldston describes it this way:

"Popular with Congress was the message Roosevelt sent on March 13, 1933. This [bill] called for amendment of the Volstead Act to permit the manufacture and sale of beer. Congress had already, in February, 1933, voted to repeal the Eighteenth (Prohibition)

Amendment. The Twenty-First (Repeal) Amendment was awaiting only the necessary approval of thirty-six states to become law. But while waiting for whiskey, the nation would have beer. Over the objections of the few die-hard 'dry' congressmen, representatives and senators added wine to beer just for good measure and chanted 'vote-vote-we want beer.' On April 7, 1933, beer was again legal in America. In New York City six heavy brewery horses pulled a bright red beer wagon up to the Empire State Building and presented Al Smith with a case of lager. In the 'beer cities,' St. Louis and Milwaukee, thousands thronged the street singing 'Sweet Adeline.' Happy days were really here again, it seemed."[4]

But at the end of 1933, there were still millions unemployed. 1934 was a dismal year, with the stock market weak. During the last half of the year some people felt that the New Deal was retreating. No new legislation of importance was proposed, and the impression was that its aggressive tactics in 1933 had pretty much failed to restore prosperity.

Early in 1935 Roosevelt proposed a gigantic new program to solve the unemployment problem, and entrusted to Presidential Assistant Harry Hopkins the responsibility of implementing it. It would cost nearly $5 billion.

Later in 1935 Roosevelt asked Congress to enact a Social Security Law. Conservatives were dumbfounded by the proposal. One prominent senator remarked, "It will take all the romance out of life."

In May, 1935, the United States Supreme Court declared the National Recovery Act unconstitutional – a deadly blow to the New Deal.

Other legislation, such as a "Soak the Rich" tax bill, had shaken the confidence of many businessmen. To many wealthy people, Roosevelt and the New Deal had become anathema. Despite this, Roosevelt overwhelmingly won reelection in 1936 over Alfred Landon of Kansas.

"New Deal measures did not end depression in the countryside. As late as 1939, little groups of migrants from midwestern dust bowls of southern poverty could be seen huddled around their broken-down cars outside gas stations on the roads that led westward. And farm prices, although they rose dramatically over their 1930 lows, never reached prosperous levels until the Second World War created a new demand for food in abundance. Nor did New Deal laws automatically save the countryside from erosion and man-made disaster. . . . But the New Deal

4. *Ibid*, p. 95

did make a start towards reform and did establish guidelines for policies which were eventually to transform both the countryside and the men who wrested a living from it."[5]

Beyond any question, the outbreak of the Second World War solved many of our economic problems, particularly unemployment. Once the majority of the fifteen million idle went to work, many of our other problems were automatically eased.

"Later in 1933 Roosevelt set out to raise the depressed level for farm commodities by deliberately cutting the dollar's purchasing power. This could be done, he thought, by decreasing the dollar's value in terms of the ounces of gold it would buy. But the price of gold was fixed by law at the gold-standard level of $20.67 an ounce, and FDR's advisers had to recommend a complex legal excuse for raising it. The President's jolly reply: 'I have a method of my own to break the law which I think is much simpler.'

"He ordered the Reconstruction Finance Corporation to set up a special office to buy corn, cotton, wheat and – gold. Each morning a few aides gathered in the President's bedroom to set the buying price, pushing it higher and higher each day. 'If anybody ever knew how we set the gold price through a combination of lucky numbers, etc., I think they would really be frightened,' noted Henry Morgenthau in his diary. The White House gold-buying team certainly frightened Montague Norman and the Bank of England, who predicted 'the whole world will be put into bankruptcy.'

"That's how the price of gold was eventually raised to the $35-an-ounce level still prevailing today as the dollar's international value. The Treasury's willingness to sell its gold to foreign governments at this price is the last active link with the gold standard of bygone days."[6]

In a sense the proponents of the New Deal adopted, from English Economist John Maynard Keynes, the philosophy of deficit financing with its optimistic notion that deficits in bad years are offset by surpluses in good years. Whatever the dangers, the idea became pretty solidly established that it was incumbent on our government to manipulate spending and fiscal controls in order to run the economy on an even keel.

What did the stock market do during this turbulent period? As seen in the chart in the beginning of Part Two, the Dow-Jones Industrial

5. *Ibid,* p. 164

6. *The Wall Street Journal,* February 19, 1965, used by permission.

Average fluctuated within a very narrow range between 1933 and 1939. To those of us in the investment business, evaluating it was elusive and difficult. Prices on the Exchange moved very little, despite all the innovations put into effect by the provisions of the New Deal.

CHAPTER FOUR

CAVEAT EMPTOR!

Legislation to form the Securities and Exchange Commission, popularly known as the SEC, was incorporated in the Securities Act of 1933 and put into effect in 1934. Without question, it was one of the most important pieces of legislation of the twentieth century. Heretofore, investors had had little or no protection, and were bilked and robbed of millions of dollars by unscrupulous crooks. In many cases, people at a higher level took advantage of investors by failing to disclose all the facts necessary to make an honest appraisal of a security.

Many persons – some of them gamblers and some who were out just to make millions regardless of tactics – used the ploy of accumulating thousands of shares of a stock and disseminating some very bullish news, many times exaggerated or untrue, about its prospects. Innocently, the public would proceed to buy it, and it would have a fantastic rise. When the insiders felt it was time to unload, they quietly liquidated and left the public holding the bag. Not only did insiders sell out at the top, but frequently they also went short, profiting dishonestly on the downside as well as the upside.

Hundreds of examples of such an operation could be cited, but perhaps one of the best-known was the Mike Meehan (and associates) pool in Radio Corporation of America. Michael J. Meehan held a seat on the New York Stock Exchange and was a specialist for Radio Corporation of America as well as several other stocks. In the early Twenties he saw the possibilities of manipulating the stock of RCA. The name was well-known, it was in an exciting field, and there was a large number of shares outstanding. Mr. Meehan had no difficulty in persuading several other well-known manipulators to join him in a pool operation. Optimistic reports were disseminated, including misrepresentations on possible earnings. The stock was in the eighties, and as soon as Meehan's group had accumulated enough stock, these misleading, bullish reports were broadcast. An unsuspecting public rushed in to buy. The stock quickly moved up to 110, with Meehan and his group selling on the way up. They probably went short some stock near the top. In any case, the bubble soon burst and the stock sold off about twenty points. The Meehan group came out with several million in profits, and the gullible public was left holding the bag in what was probably one of the most diabolically effective stock manipulations of the decade. Other well-known manipulators during this period were Jesse Livermore, Allan Ryan, Joseph P. Kennedy, John J. Raskob and Walter C. Durant.

All through the Twenties RCA stock continued to be a popular speculative vehicle. As late as 1928 it was selling under 100, but in the speculative frenzy of 1929, it went to about 500.

The original five Securities and Exchange Commissioners were appointed by President Roosevelt – Judge Ferdinand Pecora, James Landis, George C. Mathews, and Robert Healey, and to the amazement and dismay of many, Joseph P. Kennedy as Chairman. Since he was a front-running speculator and manipulator of the market, Kennedy's appointment came as a great shock to many people. He had been, as most people knew, the largest contributor to Franklin Roosevelt's campaign. But Joseph P. Kennedy reigned over the SEC for two years and did a splendid job. He was subsequently appointed U. S. Ambassador to the Court of St. James.

The Securities and Exchange Commission's duties were initially outlined in the Securities and Exchange Act of 1933; the Securities and Exchange Act of 1934 was designed to increase information available to investors and to prevent unfair practices in the securities markets. To accomplish this, stock exchanges and the over-the-counter markets were placed under the SEC's supervision. As it presently functions, the SEC:

1. Is composed of five Commissioners appointed by the President for a term of five years. One of the Commissioners is elected annually as Chairman.

2. Not only administers a number of the most important reform measures of the New Deal – the Securities Act of 1933, the Securities and Exchange Act of 1934, the Public Utility Holding Company Act of 1939, the Trust Indenture Act of 1939, the Investment Company Act of 1940 and the Investment Advisers Act of 1940 – but in addition may act as a participant in corporate reorganizations in the Federal courts under the National Bankruptcy Act.

3. Compels full disclosure to investors of material facts about securities

offered and sold in interstate commerce or through the mails. Before an issue of securities may be offered for public sale, the issuer must file with the SEC a registration statement giving complete information on such securities and on the issuing company. Dealers in securities must provide their customers with a condensation of the data in the statement. The agency examines the statement (or prospectus), and may refuse registration if it appears to be misleading or inaccurate.

4. Supervises the activities of the stock exchanges, their member firms, and these firms' employees – as well as the over-the-counter markets. Trading practices are closely regulated.

5. Controls "insiders'" use of information. Officers, directors, and principal stockholders of corporations having registered securities must report in detail their own transactions in these securities.

Following in 1940, the Investment Company and Investment Advisers Acts provided for registration and regulation of investment trusts (including mutual funds), investment companies and investment advisers.

Another area of securities dealings came under scrutiny in the early 1930's. Throughout the 1920's and until 1934, the big commercial banks in the larger cities had what were called "investment affiliates." For instance, the Guaranty Trust Company's investment affiliate was known as the "Guaranty Company of New York," and the "National City Company" was affiliated with National City Bank. They were separate corporations, and engaged in the sale and purchase of common stocks, preferred stocks, and bonds as well as the underwriting of new issues. There were absolutely no restrictions on their operations, and unusually large profits were generated. The larger affiliates had offices in several cities.

Because they were affiliated with banks, there was an assumption in the public mind that these investment affiliates would deal in sound securities. Alas, they were guilty instead of very bad judgment – especially during the 1920's, when they literally ran wild, selling securities to the public that were extremely speculative. In many instances, such as those involving foreign bonds, investors lost millions and millions of dollars. It gave the banks themselves a black name that took years to erase.

Naturally, there were people who recognized that this situation needed correcting. The very able Senator Carter Glass of Virginia was the man to set the wheels in motion. On June 16, 1933, the Glass-Steagal Banking Act was introduced (Steagal was a Representative from Alabama), and it passed without opposition. This bill separated commercial from investment banking; in the future, a bank might undertake one activity or the other. It also brought into law the Federal Deposit Insurance Corporation, whereby the Federal government insured the bank deposits of private citizens up to $10,000 (recently raised to $20,000).

The Glass-Steagal Banking Act, along with the newly-formed SEC, gave the investor protection that was long overdue!

CHAPTER FIVE

BUILDING THE PITTSBURGH CLIENTELE

Shortly after returning to Pittsburgh, I joined the Duquesne Club, undoubtedly one of America's finest businessmen's clubs. Most of the members now, as then, are prominent Pittsburgh bankers, lawyers, and industrialists. My office was in the Oliver Building diagonally across the street from the club, so I lunched there nearly every day. In the dining room where I usually ate, there was one large table seating ten or twelve men on a "first come" basis until it was filled. We got to know one another well.

One day in the Spring of 1934, I went to lunch early and found one other member at the table. He was one of Pittsburgh's best-known attorneys and a very wealthy man, a little reserved but quite urbane and attractive. As I sat down beside him he said, "Harland, I hear that the State of Pennsylvania expects to offer $200 million principal amount of bonds tomorrow with an unusually high coupon. What is your opinion of them?" I replied that while bond markets were presently chaotic, these bonds were most attractive for the long pull. He asked me to come to his office at two o'clock, where he confided, "Harland, I'm ashamed to admit it but since the Bank Holiday I've kept $1,000,000 in cash and I think now I should invest it." I agreed that both bonds and stocks were cheap.

He asked how many of these State of Pennsylvania's he should purchase. I felt that with that much uncommitted cash he should invest $200,000, whereupon he placed the order by telephone. Then he showed me a list of his other investments, saying, "I want to employ you as my Investment Counselor, and your first job will be to invest the remaining $800,000. What will your fee be?" I asked for a few minutes to study his portfolio. For the most part it was made up of good common stocks and about $500,000 in tax-exempt bonds. After looking it over carefully, I replied that the fee would be $6,000 annually. "Fine," he responded. "Now get me your recommendations as soon as you can on the investment of the cash. You have convinced me that this is the time to invest it."

Within a few days I submitted a recommendation for common

stocks such as Gulf Oil, Aluminum Company of America, Eastman Kodak, General Motors and Standard Oil of New Jersey. When the program was completed, I had a very nice client with a portfolio that was truly *crème de la crème.*

One other experience in Pittsburgh is worth recording, and it also had to do with an attorney, Mr. George P. Rhodes. We occasionally ate at the same table at the Duquesne Club. In addition to being a highly successful attorney and quite scholarly, he was an excellent bridge player. The club had a beautiful card room, and after four o'clock, bridge players usually congregated for a rubber or two before going home. I played either with or against George Rhodes frequently and got to know him well before his death in 1942. A large estate was left to his two sons and one daughter. I was asked to meet with the sons at the Duquesne Club one Sunday, where I learned that they had elected to retain me as their Investment Counselor. Each had received an identical list of securities along with a considerable amount of cash.

In Pennsylvania there was then, and still is, a four-to-eight mills tax on certain securities, and Pennsylvania residents try, as a rule, to avoid securities that are subject to this tax. Many mistakes have been made in holding too closely to this policy, and it was well illustrated in this case. The older son, living in New Jersey, could forget the restrictions of Pennsylvania. With the cash available for investment, I recommended to each son the same securities. But I recommended Polaroid to the New Jersey brother, and by mutual agreement did not buy it for the brother and sister living in Pittsburgh. All of the stocks purchased have done beautifully, but Polaroid has been sensational. Here was a case where it would have been wise to overlook the small Pennsylvania tax.

The sister was married to a very fine physician who died at an early age. Her second husband died shortly after their marriage, and finally she died prematurely. Her only child, a son, inherited her estate and today is one of my clients. The brother from Pittsburgh is also still one of my clients, but the older brother from New Jersey died of a heart attack at his Princeton reunion in 1966. I would relate how much his original Polaroid stock had grown by the time of his death, but the reader would find it hard to believe!

I had found that small banks made excellent clients, the large banks utilizing their own Investment Departments. Not being permitted to buy common stocks, they invested most of their surplus money in government and corporate bonds, and occasionally tax-exempts. By concentrating in this area I secured several small banks as clients.

One particular case is worth mentioning. This bank was in a suburb of Pittsburgh. In 1928, when things looked rosy, the directors had authorized construction of a beautiful new building. In the meantime, a poor job had been done in selecting the bank's investments, and like many banks, it experienced heavy withdrawals leading up to the Bank Holiday. As a result, it could not reopen. The Reconstruction Finance Corporation came in, bought a sizable amount of a preferred stock issue and reopened the bank with new officers and directors.

The new bank president had been a successful businessman in the area, and a former bank stockholder. He was a neighbor of ours and knew what my profession was. Soon after being made president he came to me for advice. Among the bank's assets were $500,000 of railroad bonds; their cost was the market price on the day the bank reopened. Needless to say, they were all selling at fifty cents on the dollar or less. He wondered whether to sell and break even or hold, hoping for an improvement in the market. I went over the list carefully. Most of the bonds were underlying mortgages such as Atchison Topeka and Santa Fe General 4's. One $100,000 holding was Great Northern Railway 7's of 1936, due in three years and selling at 50.

I could not believe that these good bonds would default. I reasoned that the Reconstruction Finance Corporation would come forth with help, and that perhaps we had seen the worst. So I advised their retention. The president called me the next day and asked me to meet with the board to state my reasons. This I did, and we were employed. Later, the president told me that a competing firm had recommended the sale of the bonds, and several directors favored their recommendation. But my friend held out for me and we got the account. Incidentally, the Great Northern Railway paid off the bonds in 1936 with the help of a loan from the Reconstruction Finance Corporation. All the other bonds had a splendid recovery, and the bank eventually made a handsome profit.

With the help of the RFC and the WPA, new jobs were being created, and one could see gradual improvement in the national economy. And yet, confidence was slow to return.

"Roosevelt's second inaugural address, on January 20, 1937, had included the memorable lines: 'I see one-third of a nation ill-housed, ill-clad, ill-nourished.' And as the New Deal's second term opened to the subsiding of Midwestern dust clouds and the increasing din of industrial warfare, the problem of hard-bed poverty in America seemed no nearer to a solution than it had been four years earlier."[7]

---

7. Goldston, *op cit*, p. 177

". . . Then, in August, 1937, disaster struck again. The economy suddenly tumbled. Industrial output fell overnight in the most dramatic drop in American history – worse even than the downfall of 1930. All the gains of the past were wiped out. In three months steel production fell from 80 per cent of capacity to 19 per cent. Once again the stock market plunged. And by January 1, 1938, more than two million people had been thrown out of work.

"As FDR had been willing to take credit for recovery, so now he had to shoulder responsibility for what his enemies gleefully called the 'Roosevelt recession.' And, in truth, the President had contributed to it. The prosperity of 1937 had been built upon shaky foundations. There were still seven million unemployed, and only by government deficit spending – the pouring of gigantic sums of money into the economy through relief and public works – had the semblance of prosperity been achieved. But in June of 1937, attacked once again by a wave of worry about government debt and spending, and urged by some advisers to try to balance the federal budget, Roosevelt had slashed spending to the bone. He had cut WPA rolls drastically and slowed PWA projects to a standstill. This might not have had an adverse effect on the economy if private business had been ready or able to resume investment and expansion, but in 1937 private business was still not ready to do so. Many businessmen simply had lost confidence in the economy, many more feared New Deal policies, and a few held back in a conscious effort to discredit the administration. In cutting spending Roosevelt had jovially referred to taking off 'the bandages and throwing away the crutches' to see if the patient could walk. The patient collapsed.

"Many New Dealers had been opposed to the cutback in spending. Aside from those like Hopkins and Ickes who did not like to see their own programs diminished, there were important economists who felt that it was a dangerous policy. Marriner Eccles, Governor of the Federal Reserve Board, expressed it succinctly. 'Government,' he declared, 'must be the compensatory agent in this economy; it must unbalance its budget, (spend) during deflation (when private spending sank) and create surpluses (save) during periods of great business activity.'

"While the argument raged, once again, in early 1938, many Americans came close to starvation. In Chicago, children were digging through garbage cans again; in Cleveland people fought over rotten vegetables in the streets; in the Midwest generally, WPA rolls increased by 200 per cent in six months. Cities such as Omaha, Toledo, and Chicago were once again running out of relief funds (Chicago closed down all nineteen of its relief stations). By April, 1938, the roll of the unemployed stood once again at ten million, and conservative critics of the New Deal were all but dancing in the street. The people's disaster, by seeming to prove the New Deal wrong, gladdened their hearts. And, after staving off the dire necessity as long as possible, on April 2, 1938, Roosevelt caved in and sent a new large-scale spending program to Congress. He asked for, and received, a total of $3.75 billion, to be split up between PWA, WPA, and various relief agencies. Thereafter the economy began to recover."[8]

As late as 1938, over ten million people had been unemployed. There was great uncertainty, and there is nothing worse for the stock market than uncertainty. Prices declined precipitously. In 1938, a low in the Dow-Jones Industrial Average for the decade of 93.95 was reached.

In addition to our domestic turmoil, war clouds were hanging over Europe. The Munich Pact – of complete capitulation – was signed by England's Prime Minister, Neville Chamberlain, on September 30, 1938. Hitler had summoned him and other European allied leaders to Munich for a conference, and to a man they all agreed to all of Hitler's demands. When Chamberlain returned to London after the conference, he announced to the world that he had secured "peace in our time." This period of appeasement came to be symbolized by Chamberlain and his ever-present umbrella. The Munich Pact permitted immediate occupation by Germany of the Sudetenland, but also provided for plebiscites which were never carried out. Aggressions by Germany were stepped up, and the following March Czechoslovakia was invaded.

The Second World War broke out on September 1, 1939. While we were not involved until Pearl Harbor, the invasion of the Low Countries in 1940 brought a real upheaval in our stock market. Those of us in the Investment Counseling field were in a difficult position. Since most of my clients held stocks purchased at very low prices, by and large I advised retention, although there were cases where sales were recommended.

---

8. *Ibid*, pp. 181-182

PART THREE

1940-1950

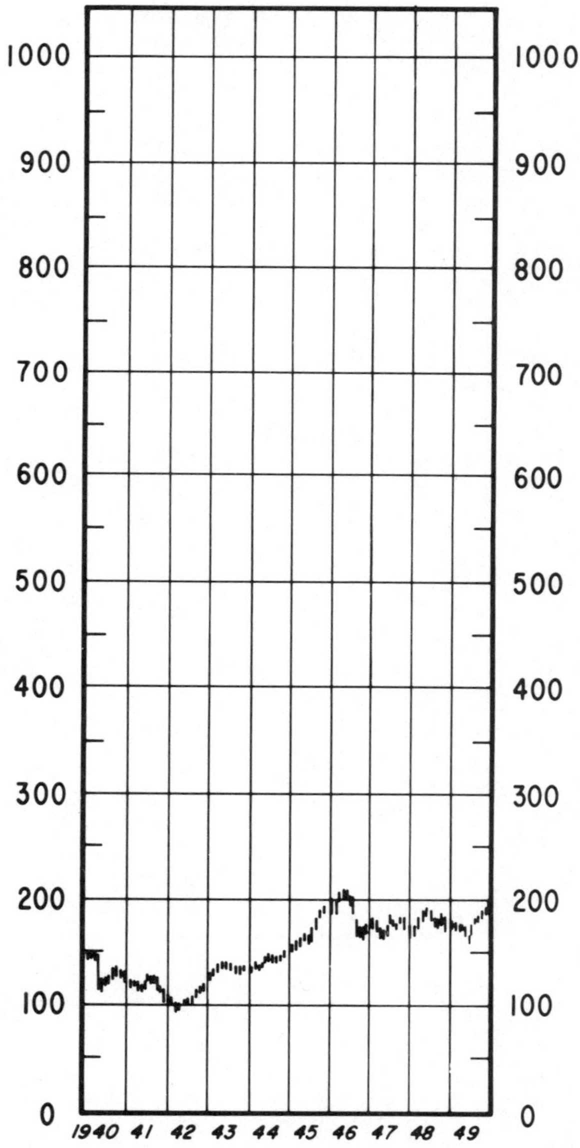

1000
900
800
700
600
500
400
300
200
100
0
1940
41
42
43
44
45
46
47
48
49

CHAPTER ONE

ATTACK!

Abraham Lincoln once said: "If we could first know where we are and whither we are tending, we could better judge what to do and how to do it." Certainly this was pertinent to the beginning of the fourth decade of the twentieth century.

On May 10, 1940, Germany began the invasion of the Low Countries. In *The Gathering Storm,* Winston Churchill had this to say: "The morning of the tenth of May dawned and with it came tremendous news. Boxes with telegrams poured in from the Admiralty, the War Office and the Foreign Office. The Germans had struck their long-awaited blow. Holland and Belgium were both invaded. Their frontiers had been crossed at numerous points. The whole movement of the German Army upon the invasion of the Low Countries and of France had begun."[1]

Continuing, he said, "Holland had been attacked without the slightest pretext or warning. The avalanche of fire and steel had rolled across the frontiers and when resistance broke out, an overwhelming onslaught was made from the air. The whole country was in a state of wild confusion."[2]

Neville Chamberlain resigned as Prime Minister and was immediately replaced by Churchill.

These dramatic events naturally brought a sharp decline in the stock market in 1940. The Dow-Jones Industrial Average sank as low as 111.84 from a recent 151 high. Many investors ran for cover, creating panicky selling. The feeling was widespread that our nation would eventually become involved. For the most part, I advised my clients to sit tight with good stocks such as General Motors, American Telephone, Standard Oil of New Jersey, and duPont, suggesting that any liquidation might be close to the bottom.

There was another plus factor that many investors overlooked. With

1. Winston S. Churchill, *The Gathering Storm.* Boston: Houghton, Mifflin Co., 1948, p. 662. Used by permission.
2. *Ibid*

the invasion of Poland in 1939, England and other European countries had started to prepare for war, calling on the United States for steel, ships, food, textiles, airplanes and other materiel. This helped our stumbling economy enormously, setting in motion the reversal upwards and out of the Depression. Industrial production would rise from 30 in 1939 to 50 at the end of 1941, and as high as 80 by the end of 1943. In the meantime, the Dow-Jones Average would climb to 140 in 1943 and to nearly 200 by 1945. Anyone who had sold stocks in 1940, with the Average at 111, would have seen the prices for his former stocks almost double by the end of the war.

During the years 1939 to 1946, the Federal Reserve discount rate wavered between ½% and 1%. Yields on high grade bonds remained at 2½% to 3%. An investor would have fared poorly in this period to place idle funds in bonds.

Despite the fact that two of his most important pieces of legislation – NRA and AAA – had been declared unconstitutional by the Supreme Court, in spite of his unpopular and unsuccessful attempts to pack the Supreme Court, and with as many as ten million unemployed as late as 1939, Franklin D. Roosevelt in 1940 retained sufficient popularity for reelection to a third term. His Republican opponent, Wendell L. Willkie, gave him a good race by polling twenty-two million votes – the largest popular vote received by a defeated candidate up to this time.

In the campaign of 1940, Franklin Roosevelt, with great emphasis, told a Boston audience, "And while I am talking to you mothers and fathers, I give you one more assurance; I have said this before, but I shall say it again and again and again. Your boys are not going to be sent into any foreign wars." Within fourteen months, American boys were fighting in Europe and Asia. Shortly after Roosevelt's election, the Selective Service Act was passed, legislating peacetime compulsory military training.

Coming with dramatic suddenness, Pearl Harbor took the entire nation by surprise, including official Washington. Security prices tumbled and the markets were chaotic. The Dow-Jones Industrial Average went as low as 92 soon after Pearl Harbor. At the beginning it appeared that the Japanese had the upper hand, and many people thought we might be defeated as we went through the agonizing days of the Bataan Death March. There were rumors that the Japanese would soon invade the harbors of Los Angeles and San Francisco. Many historians have said that they were in a position to occupy both cities, since our military forces were temporarily shattered and disorganized.

It was some months before the tide turned and we could breathe more easily.

Few realized at the time (and perhaps it was just as well) that this was the beginning of a worldwide, devastating conflict that would last until September, 1945. Nearly every major nation on the globe would be involved in one way or another in this holocaust, which would bring slaughter, famine and misery to millions of people – not to mention the destruction of many great cities. Historians have estimated that upwards of 70,000,000 men were involved in the fighting.

It had been apparent during the years 1940 and 1941 that we would eventually be drawn into the conflict. During these two years we had given substantial assistance to England and other Western powers. Since this is not intended as an historical treatise, I shall not attempt to lead my readers through the agonizing events that followed our entry into the war. However, it did unite the nation as never before and the citizenry made the sacrifices called for – food rationing, excess profits taxes, gasoline rationing, virtual closing of all automobile manufacturing plants. Insofar as possible, all industrial production was converted to the making of war materials. The moral fabric of our country was tested and not found wanting. But the cost of victory was high.

Over 15,000,000 Americans served in various branches of the service, and there were more than 1,000,000 casualties sustained in France, Germany, Italy, North Africa and the Pacific Theatre. Of this number, some 300,000 were battle deaths and approximately 700,000 wounded. In addition to casualties of the armed forces, civilian and military losses exceeded $300,000,000,000. Casualties suffered by Russia, England, Germany and Japan were much greater than ours.

By late 1942 we had made excellent progress in pushing the Japanese back in the Pacific. We had also been able to land a sizable army in North Africa and within a few months had brought a stinging defeat to Rommel and the German forces there. After this great victory, we went on to push the invasion of Italy successfully. Mussolini was forced to abdicate, and Italy joined the Western allies. President Roosevelt, Prime Minister Churchill, and Premier Stalin met at Teheran to agree on military measures designed to crush Germany.

In June, 1944, led by General Dwight D. Eisenhower, allied troops gained a foothold on the continent by way of Normandy, and pushed to the German border after several months of savage fighting. In the meantime, we had continued our successes in the Pacific and had Japan on the defensive.

In November, 1944, Franklin D. Roosevelt was reelected for his fourth term, defeating Thomas L. Dewey by a small margin.

Allied forces continued to pound the enemy mercilessly and the German surrender came at last on May 8, 1945.

Roosevelt did not live to see this final triumph of the allied nations. Shortly after noon on April 12, 1945, he died at his second home in Warm Springs, Georgia. In February he had attended the Crimean Conference along with Churchill, Stalin and other allied leaders. From pictures taken at that conference, it was obvious that he was in a declining state of health.

Roosevelt was succeeded by his Vice-President, Harry S. Truman. At the Democratic Convention in 1944, Roosevelt had expressed a preference for Henry A. Wallace, or Justice William O. Douglas, as his running mate. But the big city bosses preferred Harry Truman, and he was chosen. When he was sworn in as President, Truman was in a very difficult spot. Roosevelt had not consulted him on major domestic and foreign affairs and he entered the White House totally unprepared to cope with the many pressing problems. He humbly asked for the nation's prayers.

Truman called his program the Fair Deal. Because of the pressure of foreign problems, he was compelled to put domestic issues aside temporarily.

On August 3, 1945, a military order was issued from his office to General Carl Spaatz to deliver and drop atomic bombs on the Japanese cities Hiroshima and Nagasaki. The incredible blasts virtually knocked Japan out of the war and left the two cities practically destroyed. So great was the shock to all humanity that it would make the end of the war seem like secondary news. On August 9, 1945, a second atomic bomb was released on Nagasaki, with further disastrous results. The Japanese now knew that their position was hopeless.

Their leaders surrendered on August 14, 1945, and World War II became history. Formal surrender was made on the U. S. battleship *Missouri* in Tokyo Harbor on September 2, 1945.

The decision to drop atomic bombs on these Japanese cities was undoubtedly one of the most difficult ones a President ever had to make.

Despite the fact that Harry Truman was closely allied with the corrupt and infamous Pendergast political machine of Kansas City, he consistently maintained a record of honesty and uprightness as President. He had been elected to the United States Senate in 1934, and was reelected in 1940 in spite of the fact that the Pendergast machine had collapsed. Mr. Pendergast was convicted of income tax evasion, and served a term in prison.

Truman's first term in the Senate was not known for any brilliant achievements. But during his second term, he introduced a resolution to create a Senate Committee to act as "Watchdog" of the rearmament program. He was named Chairman of the committee. An excellent job was done, and it was recognized that the Committee's efforts saved the government several billion dollars. This investigation made the hitherto obscure Missourian a national figure.

Two significant historical events occurred in 1947. In February, when the British government announced that it could no longer afford to supply military and economic aid to Greece and Turkey, Truman immediately announced that the U. S. would take over the responsibility. This became known as the "Truman Doctrine," and with it the U. S. embarked on an ever-widening program in which we assumed the global burden England had borne since the middle of the eighteenth century.

In June, 1947, Secretary of State George C. Marshall, at Harvard University, proposed vast U. S. financial aid to restore Europe's shattered economy. Between 1948 and 1951, we spent $12,000,000,000 for European recovery under this "Marshall Plan."

In 1947, Congress passed the National Security Act, which, pursuant to the President's request, placed the Army, Navy, and Air Force under the U. S. Department of Defense.

At the Potsdam Conference following World War II, the city of Berlin was divided into two sectors, West and East, resulting in severe tensions between Russia and the Western powers. A joint allied military government was formed, but was not successful, and Russia withdrew from this alliance. In the meantime, the Western powers maintained that settlement of the Berlin problem depended on the reunification of Germany.

Differences led to a serious incident in 1948-49. The Soviet Union placed a blockade on all land and water communications between West Berlin and West Germany. Western powers, with the United States government, attempted to supply West Berlin by a vast airlift. They succeeded, and the blockade was finally withdrawn in May, 1949; the airlift ended in a few months. But tension did not disappear. Many feared that this incident might lead to an all-out war between the West and the Soviet Union, and feelings ran high for several months. Naturally, our markets were nervous and volatile during this period.

Japan's surrender in September, 1945, had been accompanied by a worldwide sense of relief and rejoicing. But it would take years to restore the damage. Housing was scarce – so were food and clothing – and many nations were haunted by inflation and economic dislocations. Needless to say, it took several years for our economy to recover, and it was not until the early Fifties that the stock market began to regain signs of stability.

CHAPTER TWO

GO WEST, YOUNG MAN

Shortly after Pearl Harbor, the firm of Lionel D. Edie & Co. offered me a position too attractive to resist. I found that they were bullish on stocks, as was I. In April of 1942, Helen and I moved our family to Montclair, New Jersey, where I prepared to take up my new duties with this splendid firm, replacing Dr. Ernest Shaw.

Lionel D. Edie & Co. had a fine research organization and the firm was well-equipped to service investors. Dr. Edie had a national reputation as an extremely able economist. To step into the shoes of his associate, Ernest Shaw, was not an easy assignment. Ernie was able, erudite, and had a delightful, outgoing personality. He had been handling some of the largest and most important clients at Edie's. I absorbed practically all of them, and had only about three weeks to meet them and familiarize myself with their investments when Ernie left for the Armed Forces. In addition, I held all of my accounts from Pittsburgh and Washington.

The recovery of the market following Pearl Harbor was very gradual and painful. All during 1942 stocks were on the bargain counter, and at Edie's we purchased aggressively. What a fortunate break for everyone, for the recovery during the next decade proved to be fantastic.

Because of my years of experience, Dr. Edie delegated some important responsibilities to me. I was placed on the Policy Committee and in a sense soon became his number two assistant. Franklin Cole, executive vice-president, was second in command.

About three months after I joined his organization, Dr. Edie called me into his office one day and said, "Ike, I am due to meet with our clients in California next week. I can't possibly make it, and Franklin Cole is unable to go. I am writing them all today to announce that you will come out as my substitute." I said that I would gladly go and do my best. Secretly, I hoped that I would not fall too far short of measuring up to Dr. Edie.

The war in the Pacific meant that plane tickets were practically impossible, and it was nearly as difficult to get train reservations. I was finally able to get an upper berth on the Burlington "Zephyr" to San

Francisco. Every available seat and berth was taken, with the majority of the passengers either servicemen bound for the Pacific or servicemen's wives on their way to join their husbands. The trip took three days and four nights. The berth underneath me (we were over the wheels) was occupied by a young mother who, with her year-old baby, was traveling to join her husband in California. The baby naturally did some crying, quite a bit of it at night. Consequently, between the baby and the upper berth over the wheels, I didn't sleep too well. The young wife had a real problem in getting to the dining car with the child. In fact, all the passengers had a real problem, and we often stood in line for an hour to receive the very mediocre food. In addition, the soldiers and sailors piled all their luggage in the men's washroom, and one could scarcely get to the wash basin or find room to shave. The mother had never traveled on a Pullman before nor eaten in a dining car. The first morning out of Chicago she asked me if I would go to the dining car with her. It was only two cars ahead, and I suggested that I watch her baby while she went to breakfast. I assured her that I could manage, as we had reared four children. She gratefully accepted my offer, and for the remainder of the trip, I took charge of the baby three times a day while the mother went to the diner. At long last, her husband met her in Oakland.

I ferried over to San Francisco. I was thrilled, not only because this was my first trip to California, but also because I eagerly anticipated my meetings with this prominent group of men, composed of bank and insurance company presidents as well as heads of large corporations such as Standard Oil of California. I had a reservation at the Fairmont, knowing that the meeting was to be held at a club directly across the street. Of course, Dr. Edie had gone over the list of men who would attend, but I had never met any of them.

We had a delicious lunch, and then I held forth. I was a little nervous, although I don't think it showed. I spoke for about thirty minutes, outlining our policy and discussing the economic situation, making some comments on certain corporations, and ending with the thought that we were very bullish on stocks despite the death struggle with Japan and Germany. At the time of my visit, the Dow-Jones Industrial Average was still between 100 and 120.

For an hour these able and experienced men shot questions at me on individual companies. What could be expected in the way of increased taxes? What did we think about many other things that would influence the price of stocks? After weathering this session successfully, I felt ready for anything.

I left San Francisco that night for Los Angeles, where two meetings were scheduled on successive days. Here again I was confronted by a very knowledgeable group, successful men who were bankers, brokers, insurance company executives and industrialists. At both meetings I was able to continue the pattern established in San Francisco. Naturally, I was elated that I could live up to the level – or approach it – that had been established by Dr. Edie.

But my big thrill was just ahead. Of the individual clients in Los Angeles, two were internationally-known movie actresses. I cannot name them – both are still living – but they were beautiful, gracious ladies who lived in great luxury in Beverly Hills, each house replete with a large staff of servants. My visits with them were extremely fascinating. Both were happily married, and the husbands proved to be just as gracious as the ladies. I spent perhaps two or three hours with each one, highlighting my time in Los Angeles.

There remained one additional lady client in Pasadena – not a movie actress, but beautiful and charming. Her home was of Mediterranean design, and furnished with many rare Spanish and Indian pieces. Her son was an archeologist and a connoisseur of Spanish and Indian art. Many of her possessions were things he had found on expeditions to Mexico, Honduras and other Central and South American countries. I found Emily Boxley to be gracious and hospitable. She is still a client, and on my trips to see her, she always insists that Helen and I stay with her. Her son and lovely daughter are now clients, and it has been one of the nicest and most rewarding relationships I have ever had.

The next day I had reservations for my return to New York and left, feeling that my first trip to California had been quite satisfactory. I have since returned to California perhaps a hundred times, and I find it more fascinating on each visit.

Before the arrival of the nonstop prop planes, Helen and I would go to California by train, taking the Sante Fe "Super Chief" and the Burlington "Zephyr" through scenic Colorado, Utah, and the beautiful Feather River Canyon in northern California. We found this trip to be a thriller, with the train at one moment at an elevation of 8000 feet, surrounded by ice and snow, and then rapidly descending. Within an hour we would emerge into the fantastically beautiful San Joaquin Valley with its myriad flowers, orange trees heavy with fruit, and green pastures.

On several occasions we ended our visit in San Francisco by taking the beautiful daylight ride on the Southern Pacific past Mt. Shasta to Portland and Seattle, and then home via the Great Northern or

Northern Pacific. We experienced an amusing incident on one such trip.

Helen has never paid much attention to the business of securities or investments, despite the fact that she has been exposed to these things constantly for fifty years. Her main interests revolve around her home, books, her children and grandchildren, and her gardens. She has a general idea of our income and a smattering of knowledge of our securities. However, she had heard me speak enough about B.M.T. (Brooklyn Manhattan Transit), P.R.T. (Philadelphia Rapid Transit), and I.R.T. (Interboro Rapid Transit) to get the impression that all three letter symbols meant traction stocks.

We took the "Zephyr" on one of our transcontinental trips and decided to go to the dining car for dinner as early as possible upon leaving Chicago. We were seated at a table for four. Soon the car filled, and an exceptionally nice-looking couple was seated with us. We soon introduced ourselves, and within an hour were on very friendly terms. When the wife learned of my profession, she asked me what I thought of several stocks – obviously ones they owned. I gave my opinion briefly, which wasn't difficult because they were mostly blue chips. Finally she said, "Mr. Hoisington, how do you regard IBM?" Naturally I said I thought it most attractive, and had purchased it for most of my clients. Whereupon Helen said in great amazement, "Buddy, you don't recommend *traction* stocks to your clients, do you?" Of course, I quickly corrected her impression.

In the past few years we have bypassed train travel for the faster jet planes. I flew in Naval Aviation during World War I, and still love to fly. I am never happier than when we board a 707 for California. In 1969, we traveled for the first time on one of the big Super DC8's, and I was as thrilled as any youngster taking his first ride in a plane. Our visit there by means of the giant 747 in 1970 was an even bigger thrill.

Over the years, I acquired new clients in San Francisco and Rancho Sante Fe, and our oldest son moved to Carmel in 1947. Thus, we had several reasons for going to California frequently. Often we remain for two weeks or a month, and have taken time out to visit Yosemite, the Redwood Forests, the High Sierras in Mono County, Carmel, Monterey, Big Sur and many other places of interest.

One would have to go a long way to find a nicer person than one of my Rancho Santa Fe clients. She has been with me for over twenty years, and both Helen and I thoroughly enjoy her. She recently built a lovely new house with a magnificant view of the mountains, and refers to it as the "House that Harland Built" because of my management of her funds. We first met in 1950. I was bullish then on stocks and have been ever since. With that kind of policy, we were sure to get good results.

CHAPTER THREE

THE COLE-HOISINGTON REPORT

In 1944, after two and one-half years with Lionel D. Edie, I made a move that, only shortly afterward, seemed very foolish. I had not realized it in the beginning, but Dr. Edie and Franklin Cole, his executive vice-president, frequently clashed on policy procedures, on the selection of securities, and other matters. Before I realized it, the feeling between them was quite strained.

Early in 1944, Franklin confided in me that he was leaving the Edie organization to form his own firm. He had quite a following, was a super salesman, and said that three or four of the key men at Lionel Edie's had agreed to go with him. He invited me to come along and be second in command in a firm to be known as Cole, Hoisington & Co. There was to be plenty of capital; a nice space at 120 Broadway had been rented; and he offered me a handsome salary in addition to stock ownership. It all sounded very appealing and I accepted his offer. Dr. Edie made me a flattering counter-offer, but I had already made up my mind and declined.

We opened our office with a great flourish and seemed to be headed into a very beautiful situation. Along with Franklin's big following, I had some good clients, and the other Edie men brought some with them. Franklin delegated some heavy responsibilities to me. I had a sizable number of clients to supervise; in addition, he depended on me to organize our Research Department, and supervise the other account executives. We had one large department store chain that came to us for economic guidance. This latter assignment was a big one and took considerable time. But the fee, happily, was commensurate with the work involved.

On January 16, 1945, *The Wall Street Journal* carried an article headlined:

BAN ON "FLOOR TRADING" ASKED
BY SEC UNIT
Proposal Would End Such Transactions
on Two New York Exchanges

In its complaint, the SEC's Trading and Exchange Division specifically sought the abolition of "floor trading" – the buying and selling by a member for his own account which is initiated by that member while he is physically on the Exchange Floor. Floor trading, the report stated, was the single most important cause of the price rise and tremendous increase in volume of certain low-priced motor shares cited as examples.

In letters to Emil Schram and Fred C. Moffat, presidents respectively of the New York Stock Exchange and the New York Curb Exchange, the Commission asked for comments on the proposed rule not later than January 27.

In view of what has happened since in the way of trading volume, price gyrations, and public speculation in a wide variety of "glamor" stocks, the concern of the SEC over what was happening in 1944 seems greatly overdone. But at the time it created quite a furor.

Emil Schram was disturbed by the charges, and felt that the opinion of a professionally competent and respected outside organization should be obtained. He came to Franklin Cole, whom he had known for many years, for advice.

After reading the full text of the charges, we advised Mr. Schram to request a ninety-day extension of the deadline for reply to the SEC, allowing a thorough study of the situation to be made. The extension was granted, and research began immediately.

Franklin and I realized that we had assumed responsibility for a major assignment which would require the coordinated efforts of many qualified people, both within our organization and from the outside. Mr. Schram agreed to our proposed plan of procedure. Compilation and analysis of the data necessary for arriving at a reasoned judgment on the questions raised by the SEC proposal, and preparation of a report setting forth our opinions and recommendations, took place over the ensuing two and a half months. This involved many man-hours of time and effort, and included visits to the Floor of the Exchange to facilitate interviews with specialists, traders, Exchange officers and partners of member firms, as well as consultations with other interested individuals and institutions. The Exchange itself, through the offices of Mr. Edward C. Gray, vice-president, provided when and as requested great quantities of statistical and other factual material bearing on the questions under study.

Prefacing our final fifty-page report to the New York Stock Exchange was a letter directed to Mr. Schram, which read in part:

"Pursuant to your request of January 25, 1945, we have undertaken a study of floor trading on the New York Stock Exchange. This study has been conducted from an objective point of view. You have asked us to examine floor trading impartially, and to report our complete findings, without minimizing any unfavorable aspect which our study might develop, and without over-emphasis upon such favorable aspects as are present. This is the attitude which we have adopted. . . .

"In undertaking our analysis, our primary objective has been to determine the extent to which floor trading contributes to, or detracts from, liquidity, continuity and orderliness in stock trading. We have employed the following methods in conducting our investigation:

1. First we have familiarized ourselves with previous studies of this subject, including those made by the New York Stock Exchange and the Securities and Exchange Commission.

2. Through personal observation on the Floor of the New York Stock Exchange we have followed the activities of floor traders and other members on a number of occasions and under varying conditions.

3. We have prepared, or have had prepared under our direction, a considerable number of statistical studies, designed to indicate the influence of floor trading on specific stocks and groups of stocks of a representative character, and under diverse conditions.

"As a result of our study, we have come to the following conclusions:

1. In many instances floor trading has made a definite and worthwhile contribution to the liquidity, continuity and orderliness of stock market trading.

2. In some cases floor trading has brought about or contributed to an artificial stimulation of market activity. This has sometimes resulted in an exaggeration or distortion of normal price trends, to the detriment of the interests of the investing public.

3. On balance, floor trading has made a constructive contribution to market liquidity, continuity and orderliness.

4. Floor trading should not be abolished. Effort should be made to direct it into channels where its influence will become more heavily weighted in the public good than may now be the case. Important potentialities along these lines appear to exist. Because of this belief, our report contains a number of suggestions which are recommended for your study and consideration. . . ."

Remarking subsequently about the SEC's charges, the report went on to state:

"On January 15, 1945, the Trading and Exchange Division of the Securities and Exchange Commission made public a report, addressed to the Commission, on floor trading. It is our opinion that this report performed a public service to the extent that it pointed out instances in the past where floor trading was conducted in such a manner that the activity of 'off the Floor' speculators appears to have been stimulated, and price trends accentuated. It is our further opinion, however, that this report performed a public disservice to the extent that it attempted to draw sweeping conclusions from an inadequate, unrepresentative base, and to the extent that the material presented is not complete and contains distortions and unsupported conjecture.

"It is not the purpose of our study to undertake a point by point discussion of this January 15, 1945, report. It is, rather, our purpose to conduct an impartial and objective study of floor trading. As an element in this study we have given careful consideration to the material contained in the Trading and Exchange Division's report. As indicated above, we are in agreement with the report on certain points, such as the undesirable effects of certain floor trading activity which took place last summer in the low-priced motor stocks. We believe that steps should be taken to prevent a recurrence of situations of this sort, and in Part Three of our analysis suggestions are made which it is hoped may be helpful in the further consideration of this subject which we believe should take place.

"However, there is much in the January 15, 1945 report with which we cannot agree. Our chief points of disagreement may be grouped under two headings, as follows:

1. The material presented is unrepresentative and inadequate. It does not form a sufficiently broad base of experience to warrant any sweeping or basic conclusions as to all of the members' 'on Floor' activities, customarily lumped together under the head of 'floor trading.'
2. The material presented is incomplete and unbalanced. It is presented in a manner which, although superficially convincing, is dangerous and in some instances, so it seems to us, unfair."

Cole, Hoisington disagreed with the reasons advanced by the SEC for its conclusions. These were perfectly valid if one accepts their premise of how to measure the effect of individual transactions on price trends – i.e., net purchases or sales of a group of traders on arbitrarily selected dates, and the relation of these changes in positions to changes in prices. The Cole-Hoisington report approached the question from an entirely different point of view, demonstrating that the effect of specific purchases or sales could best be determined by relating the price at which these transactions took place to the immediately preceding transaction – that is, the "tick" method of determining price trend. Given these basic differences between the SEC and Cole, Hoisington in the premises employed, it is not surprising that, using the same trading data, the two organizations came up with opposite conclusions. The underlying question with which both groups concerned themselves was not, "Is floor trading good or bad?" but rather, "What is the correct technique for determining the effect of individual sales and purchases on changes in the price of stocks?" Along that line, it is interesting that current technical studies of market trends seem to place increasing emphasis on the significance of transaction-by-transaction price changes – that is, "up ticks" and "down ticks."

In May of 1944, a hearing on our report was held at the SEC headquarters in Philadelphia (they had moved to Philadelphia from Washington during World War II). Our recommendations on the whole were accepted and floor trading was continued, with some basic restrictions.

CHAPTER FOUR

NEW YORK TO PRINCETON

Our first year at Cole, Hoisington & Co. was quite satisfactory, but I soon learned that our capital position was not nearly as strong as it should be. I learned, too, that Franklin and I often disagreed on policy and procedures, and by the end of the second year I was fairly dissatisfied.

The turning point came in the Fall of 1946. I took my vacation in August, and we had agreed prior to my departure that in view of market uncertainties our policy for the foreseeable future would be one of caution; we would hold our cash reserves on the theory that stocks could likely be purchased at lower levels. We had several clients in California, and while I was vacationing in August, Franklin made a trip west to call on them. I never knew exactly what brought about the change in his thinking, but he completely reversed our policy, said we were very bullish, and had our California clients put their entire cash reserves into the market.

We both returned the latter part of August. When he told me what he had done I was surprised and annoyed, but tried to take it as philosophically as possible. The day after Labor Day the market entered into a severe decline. Our California clients were naturally very unhappy. For the next three weeks, Franklin did his best to placate them, but it was obvious that they were not appeased, and it was safe to think that we would lose some business.

Franklin was not anxious to face them. Early in October, he suggested that it might be a good idea for me to go out and smooth things over. Naturally, I wasn't too enthusiastic about the prospect of facing irate clients while trying to make it appear that there was no disagreement in the firm. I well recall that it was not a pleasant trip. I stayed a week and mended fences as best I could. Up to this point, none of the clients had cancelled and I breathed a sigh of relief, because most of them were sizable accounts.

I returned on the Union Pacific, reaching Salt Lake City early in the morning of the first day out of Los Angeles. Most of the second day was spent crossing Wyoming. While there was a great deal of scenic beauty, the train trip was rather monotonous, and I settled down to some serious thinking. I was greatly disturbed. Why in the world should I mend fences for other people? Why didn't I take my clients and establish my own firm in Princeton, where we were living? A great load was suddenly lifted from my shoulders, because I realized that this was the wise, sensible thing to do. I was so eager to reach New York and break the news to Franklin that the train seemed to crawl even more slowly for the balance of the journey.

I spent the remainder of the trip compiling names of the clients I hoped would stay with me, estimating what my total gross would be and the details of how much office space and help I would need. On paper it worked out nicely, and while my income might be cut slightly in the beginning, I felt confident that new clients would be forthcoming.

I reached our office at 120 Broadway about 10:00 a.m. Through his secretary I made a luncheon date with Franklin. I got to the point immediately, indicating my decision to withdraw from Cole, Hoisington effective December 31, 1946, take my clients, and open my own office in Princeton. He was flabbergasted, and for the rest of the day tried to persuade me to change my mind, but I refused. I took an early train home to break the news to Helen. After telling her briefly of my decision and the reasons behind it, I found her to be just as enthusiastic about it as I was.

Everything developed nicely and my office in Princeton was opened formally on January 2, 1947. I was fifty years old and had always worked for large organizations. I could not be sure, of course, that my clients would all approve of the move. New York was the recognized financial center of the nation. Could an Investment Counselor function successfully from Princeton? I knew that he could, but would my clients have reservations? Fortunately, they felt as I did – that in Princeton, in a quiet atmosphere and away from the tension of Wall Street, one might, in fact, function even better than in New York. Besides, most of them felt they would love to have an excuse to visit the charming city of Princeton, and I have always encouraged them to do so. This was twenty-six years ago, and there hasn't been a day that I regretted the move.

Office space was very scarce. The only space available on Nassau Street was the third floor of the Princeton Bank and Trust Company. The space was adequate, but there was no elevator – only two very long flights of stairs. However, the rent was reasonable. Helen helped me furnish the office tastefully. The cashier who had worked for me at Cole, Hoisington came with me, and I hired two secretaries.

I had not thought of it previously, but I was the only Investment Counselor in Princeton. While I knew only a few prominent Princeton men – and Investment Counselors at that time did not advertise – my business started to grow immediately. I was amazed and pleased. Soon my son, Harland, Jr., joined me. He had been working in the New York office of Drexel & Co.

Before long we needed more space and more help. One of the secretaries, Ann Lyons, had lived in Princeton all her life, and she and her sister owned the building next door to the Princeton Bank and Trust Company. There were stores on the first floor and apartments on the second and third. I told Ann that I would gladly rent half of the second floor and convinced her that she could receive substantially more income by leasing the second and third floors to businessmen. She saw the light, and on January 1, 1949, we moved into our new quarters at Ten Nassau Street. There was a nice large room in front facing Nassau Street, a somewhat smaller one with bath and a kitchenette in the middle, and a back room with bath that made a pleasant private office for me. Incidentally, the front office had been Woodrow Wilson's law office at one time, and his voting address. In one of the desks I found an invitation to his inauguration as Governor of New Jersey.

Although my office was in the rear, I kept a desk out front where I had a lovely view of Nassau Street, probably one of the most historic streets in America, where

–towers dream against the sky,
While round them swirl and laugh and beat
The tides of youth in Nassau Street.

In Princeton the word "Nassau" predominates – Nassau Street, Nassau Hall, The Nassau Club, the stirring Princeton song, "Going back, going back, going back to old Nassau."

Nassau Hall, one of the most historic and beautiful college buildings in America, was erected in 1754-56 and named in 1756 in honor of William of Nassau, Prince of Orange, William III of England, "Champion of British Liberties."

Back and forth along Nassau Street itself the footsteps and voices of some of our greatest historic figures have been heard. Paul Revere came plowing through the mud of Nassau Street in December, 1773, on his way to Philadelphia. Several times in 1774 and 1775 he passed by again bearing dispatches for Congress. Washington's defeated Army hurried past in December, 1776 – only to return victorious a month later. The British and Hessians also marched through in 1776; Washington and Rochambeau with their armies in 1781, heading to Yorktown; and Anthony Wayne with his mutinous men in 1781. The frightened Continental Congress found refuge here in 1783. That summer, while the first foreign minister formally accredited to the United States was welcomed by Congress in Nassau Hall the happy tidings of the signing of the definitive Treaty of Peace were brought in by special courier. General Washington passed through again more than once after the Revolution, the first of eighteen Presidents of the United States, such as Thomas Jefferson, John Adams, and James Madison, who have at various times strolled along Nassau Street.

Nearly fifty years after he had fought in the Battle of Princeton, Lafayette twice stopped here on his triumphal tour of the United States. In 1836, the funeral procession of a former Vice-President of the United States, Colonel Aaron Burr, passed from Nassau Hall down to the cemetery on Witherspoon Street.

As my years in Princeton passed, I was to have the privilege of getting to know such greats as Albert Einstein, Robert Oppenheimer, Harold Dodds, Edwin Corwin, Carlos Baker, Henry Savage, Cyril Black, George Kennan and Edward Sampson. Truly I was a lucky man to be here, and away from the tension of Wall Street.

Since I was acquainted with only a few people in Princeton, I opened my office realizing that the knowledge of an Investment Counselor's arrival in town would have to spread by word of mouth. One of my acquaintances proposed me for membership in the Nassau Club, a luncheon club formed in 1890 primarily for members of the Princeton University faculty. Prominent men such as Grover Cleveland and Woodrow Wilson had been members and had served as presidents of the club. As time went on, it was discovered that to operate successfully, membership had to be opened to businessmen – and eventually to ladies. By the time I joined in 1947, about one-half of the membership was composed of faculty members and the balance of prominent businessmen.

When I opened by office in Princeton in January of 1947, I had about seventeen accounts paying total annual fees of approximately $25,000. Most of these were old accounts from Pittsburgh and Washington, in addition to a few clients who had followed me from Lionel D. Edie and Cole, Hoisington. When we moved into our new quarters at Ten Nassau Street in 1949, our business had increased considerably, requiring an office force of eight people. The new business came principally from Princeton and Wilkes-Barre, with some from Florida and California. Naturally, I was gratified. I had been right on the market and could see that business would continue to grow. As a matter of interest, the following figures are included to indicate our growth in Princeton in the fifteen year segment from 1947 to 1961:

Year	Annual Fees	Growth Over Prior Year
1947	$ 24,980	
1948	30,491	22.0%
1949	31,314	2.7%
1950	38,256	22.0%
1951	53,328	39.4%
1952	66,707	25.0%
1953	72,973	9.3%
1954	82,309	12.8%
1955	96,468	17.2%
1956	113,355	17.5%
1957	120,212	5.8%
1958	129,880	8.3%
1959	140,600	7.7%
1960	159,926	14.2%
1961	180,000	12.5%

I have had clients in fifteen states, from Maine to California in the West and to Florida in the South, as well as in Austria, France and Greece. Over seventy percent of them have been women who were divorced or widowed.

CHAPTER FIVE

SOME OF THE LADIES IN MY LIFE

SARA EVANS KENT

Of all my clients, I think I would have to select Sara Kent as the most fascinating. She wasn't the wealthiest, but from many points of view, she was the most challenging. The daughter of a Baptist minister, she was born and reared in Columbus, Georgia. Although she spent most of her adult life in the North, to the end she retained her soft Southern voice and was a true Southerner at heart. She loved hot weather and resided in the South as much as possible.

Because of his occupation, her father was never possessed of wealth. The family learned to be careful with money, and although they lived comfortably and their home was a charming one, the emphasis was on frugality. Her father was a successful minister and educator. His various posts were in well-known churches that paid higher than average salaries. Because of this, and because of a small family inheritance, Sara was sent north to Smith College for her education. Having been born with a defective hip (she needed to wear one especially-built shoe to make both legs the same length), she walked with an obvious limp and with the help of a cane.

To say that Sara was bright, vivacious and determined is putting it mildly. Perhaps her physical handicap compelled her to excel in everything she did. Excel she did, scholastically, athletically and in graciousness. At Smith, she was tennis champion and an expert horsewoman.

I first met Sara in Wilkes-Barre, Pennsylvania, where she had met and married one of that city's most charming gentlemen, Ned Kent. I had known Ned through my association with a local bank, where he was an officer and director. By this time they were middle-aged, and Ned had accumulated a tidy sum of money. Having witnessed firsthand some of my work with his bank, he told Sara that they should employ me as their own Investment Counselor. Up to this point, I had never met her.

Ned arranged for a luncheon meeting one day at the Westmoreland Club in downtown Wilkes-Barre. He had not apprised me of her physical handicap, and I was a little startled when she appeared. I learned later that each succeeding year aggravated her crippled condition. Sara and I shared a rapport and liked one another from the moment we met.

I was employed by the Kents, and the association proved to be as rewarding and pleasant as any I ever had.

Ned was stricken with a cancerous condition soon after our meeting. Unfortunately, it was incurable, and he suffered the agonies of dying slowly for two years. Blood transfusions, sedatives and everything known to the medical profession kept him alive much too long. Resembling a living skeleton when he died, Ned was smiling and outwardly cheerful to the very end.

Sara soon moved south, choosing Key West because of the warm climate and relatively modest living expense. She became quite popular there, and Helen and I visited her frequently. Her close friends were few, but chosen with care. Ernest Hemingway's first wife, Lillian (then divorced), was one of her intimate friends. Another was Marjorie Smith, a lovely and beautiful girl from New England, who had experienced an unfortunate marriage and divorce. Seeking seclusion, Marjorie came to Key West and took an important assignment with Naval Intelligence. Both Sara and we learned to love her. In addition to her striking beauty, she displayed culinary talents *par excellence.* Her seafood dinners with yellowtail as the main dish were superb. Unfortunately, Marjorie died of a heart attack aboard a plane when she and Sara were enroute to Nassau on vacation.

Another close acquaintance was "Sully" – a Mr. Sullivan who had come to Key West from Massachusetts. An artisan at iron work by trade, Sully's Irish dialect and warm personality made him a most engaging person. He built a circular iron stairway for Marjorie, leading to the second floor, which was a thing of beauty.

Neither Sully nor Marjorie had an excess of worldly goods, and Sara saw a chance to be helpful as well as natively frugal. In Key West *The New York Times* Sunday edition was 75 cents. Sara subscribed and each contributed one-third. They met regularly at Sara's on Sunday morning, where she kept the Financial and Garden Sections. Sully took the part he liked and so did Marjorie. During the week they exchanged, so that by week's end each person had received and read the full *Sunday New York Times* with a minimum outlay of capital.

Sara was priceless in more ways than one. Her letters to me were filled with sage advice and with some original expressions. At one time, when the stock market was boiling, she wrote: "Dear Holland: (as she pronounced it) What is going to stop this speculation? It is frightening. I do believe that if the U. S. Government would replace all mail boxes with slot machines, we could liquidate the national debt in a year."

She seldom failed to follow my advice, and the only time she did was pretty costly to her. I had purchased 200 shares of Texas Instruments at 25, when Texas Instruments was a fledgling company. Within two years the stock sold at 250. She was fascinated and enamored with it. Finally, I told her, "Sara, this stock has gone up too high and too fast. Let's take our profit and put the proceeds in IBM – a much more solid company." "No, Holland," she replied, "I am going to stay with Texas Instruments." Texas Instruments eventually went down to 75, while IBM's spectacular rise is history.

Three or four years prior to her death in 1963, I persuaded Sara to rewrite her will and create a trust for a niece. She had changed residence, the value of her securities had tripled, and by setting up a certain kind of trust she could probably save her estate $50,000 in taxes. She agreed.

I told Sara that I always advised my clients to counsel with G. Dykeman Sterling in Princeton, a true professional in estate planning. To Sara's first question, "How much does he charge?" I replied that not only were his charges reasonable, but he could handle everything by correspondence. She employed Dyke, and he did a masterful job. It took several months of correspondence with Sara and her attorney, but the document was eventually finalized to everyone's satisfaction. Sara, as is true with most laymen, didn't clearly understand some of the legal phraseology, and the will, of course, was fairly lengthy and wordy. We assured her that it was properly executed and was exactly the instrument she needed, and she signed it with a sense of great relief. In due course she received a bill from Dyke Sterling, and when she sent a check to Dyke, it was accompanied by the following letter:

Dear Mr. Sterling:

I am deeply grateful for your help in this matter of setting up a trust fund for my niece. It seems a small amount of money after all the taxes etc. will have been paid, and I hope she will try to build the principal again to the point where the income really amounts to something. There has been so much discussion of my death and who predeceases whom that I sometimes wonder whether I ought to stay alive and healthy. Everyone seems so set and ready to function, it seems a pity to keep them in a state of suspense.

Enclosed is my check and my thanks. I also hope we can have the pleasure of meeting some day. If not here at least on the other side of the River Styx. If you are the predecessor, leave word with Charon.

Sincerely,

Sara Evans Kent

November 1, 1961

Sara died in 1963 from cancer. Like Ned, she knew several months in advance that death was near, but she never complained and to the end was a cheerful, brave, and courageous lady. I felt a great personal loss.

JUDITH BABCOCK

Judith was a client of mine for about fifteen years. Beautiful, gracious and gentle, "Judy," as everyone affectionately called her, was the perfect client. A fascinating novel could be written about her life. She had a real tragedy when her husband divorced her after about twenty years of marriage, but I never heard her utter one word of criticism about him.

Judy was born and reared in a well-known midwest city of fairly well-to-do parents. Her father was a doctor. She and her husband, John, were childhood sweethearts, and were married shortly after their high school graduation. John was handsome, personable and ambitious. He started to work immediately as a salesman for one of our largest industrial corporations. From the very beginning he produced great results and was always number one in sales volume. His company recognized his outstanding ability, and after about three years gave him an agency in Philadelphia that included southeastern Pennsylvania and two or three counties across the river in New Jersey. Judy and John bought a house in Ardmore and on the surface they appeared to have a perfect marriage. Life was beautiful.

From the very beginning John obtained fantastic results in his business. He was on a commission basis and the money simply rolled in. For several years Judy and John enjoyed this prosperity. They soon bought a new house in a nicer location, traveled abroad, and spent their summers on a ranch in Montana. They became well-known and well-liked in suburban Philadelphia society. Life was really good – at least on the surface.

To Judy's consternation she learned that John had fallen in love with another woman. He asked for a divorce. Like the wise woman she was, Judy finally realized that it would be futile to oppose him. John naturally agreed to a very handsome alimony settlement. Her lawyer drew up the necessary papers and an agreement that Judy would receive a fair share of John's estate upon his death.

For several months Judy kept to herself and analyzed her future. She and John had spent some summers in Manchester, Vermont, and she loved the beautiful scenery of that area. She went to Manchester in June and decided to buy some property and build a house to her own taste. She finally located a ten-acre piece of property on a mountainside from which there was a magnificent view. Before starting to build, she paid a visit to some friends in Concord, Massachusetts. There she found the house she wanted – a beautiful white clapboard colonial, and one of the oldest residences in Concord. It had been used for years as an inn, and was for sale. She bought it, had it carefully torn down and moved it lock, stock and barrel to be rebuilt in Manchester exactly as it had been in Concord.

The house contained beautiful mantels and fireplaces; the lovely wainscoting in the dining room, center hall and living room were too beautiful for words. It was perfect for the location, and stands today as one of the showplaces in Vermont. Judy was a great lover of flowers and within three or four years her gardens were visited by hundreds of people, many of them members of the Vermont Garden Society. To attempt to describe her house and gardens is beyond me. One had to see them to be able to appreciate them. In addition to the flower gardens, the acreage was covered here and there with clumps of beautiful white birches. To the east a beautiful spring came out of the mountain; she featured in this spot a lovely pond, with water running rapidly through some great boulders. Lovely wild flowers graced the banks and a most artistic summer house or pagoda, complete with outdoor fireplace, was placed appropriately above the pool. I have spent many hours in that spot, thinking and dreaming and drinking in the beauty. It was a good place to get next to God. And have a martini.

Just beyond the pagoda stood one of the largest and most beautiful elms in America. It was a majestic specimen, and many nationally-known magazines asked Judy's permission to photograph it. I have a color picture of this spot, including the elm, that is a real treasure. I wish I could reproduce it in these pages.

I first met Judy about 1949. Helen and I frequently spent our summer vacations in the Manchester area, and were introduced to her by some mutual friends. We were invited to her house for cocktails one beautiful summer day. We were dazzled by the home's serenity and beauty. I did not know this until Judy told me years later, but she said to herself on meeting me, "Someday I want that man as my Investment Counselor."

Judy's former husband, John, died about 1951 and left her a very sizable portion of his estate, much of it in cash. She immediately called me, said she would like to employ me, and wanted to come to Princeton for a conference. Naturally, I was delighted to have her as a client. Everything went smoothly.

Judy, as I have said, was an ideal client. We established a custodian account and she gave me discretion to run it. She always called me "Ike," and made comments like, "Ike, I employed you because I have complete confidence in you and I know nothing about securities. So everything is in your lap." Well, with that kind of confidence and cooperation one always does a better job than with someone who might ask, "Why do you want to buy General Motors instead of Ford?" Or, "Why did you buy that stock last week when now it is off two points? Why didn't you wait and get it cheaper?" Or, "Why did you sell this stock just before it went ex-dividend? If you had waited three weeks I would have received the next dividend."

Judy always made her income meet her expenses, and, in fact, consistently saved some of her income. She retained her checking account with one of Philadelphia's largest banks, and at her death had a very substantial amount in it.

About two years after Judy became a client, she called me one day from Manchester and asked, "Ike, why do you show only 1,000 shares of Phillips Petroleum on my appraisal when I have 1,800 shares?" I replied that I would look into the matter and report back. Our records showed that Judy had given us only 1,000 shares originally, as per our evaluation. I called her and reported this. "But," she said, "I get dividends on 1,800 shares." I replied that we only collected dividends on 1,000 shares. "Oh," she said apologetically, "I forgot to tell you, Ike, I get a dividend here at home for 800 shares."

This, of course, was proof that 800 additional shares were issued in her name, and I inquired whether she had looked in her safe at home and in her safe deposit box in Philadelphia. She knew it wasn't in Philadelphia, but said that she would go through her safe, which she did; but no Phillips Petroleum. I thought eventually it would turn up, and hesitated to put up a substantial bond as yet in order to get a new certificate. On my next trip to Manchester I, too, went through the safe carefully and the desk – no Phillips. We eventually bought the bond, got a new certificate, and that was that.

We spent many happy hours with Judy in Manchester, both summer and winter. She loved having us and we loving being there. Her home was so tastefully and exquisitely decorated, and completely restful and serene. I sometimes felt that she expected John to return to her someday, but of course he never did.

Unfortunately, Judy was stricken with a fatal illness early in 1965. For almost two years she was confined alternately to her bed and to the hospital. I had had her will rewritten two years prior to her illness. As usual, Dyke Sterling and my attorney, Hugh Wise, prepared the document. She was to stop in Princeton to sign it on her way to Phoenix, Arizona, where she and a lady friend were driving to spend the winter. Her friend was not too cooperative, and requested us to meet them at the Hightstown exit to the New Jersey Turnpike, about ten miles from Princeton, for the signing. I agreed that we could, but witnesses were needed, so Hugh, my secretary, Barbara Clare, and I took a taxi and met them at the specified spot, where the will, in which I was named executor, was finalized.

Around the first of November, 1966, Sybil Nickel, Judy's companion of many years, called me and said that Judy had taken a sudden turn for the worse. She very much wanted to see me. We voted early November fourth and then started for Manchester, arriving early enough to see Judy briefly that evening. She had a very bad color and her voice was weak. When I went to her bedside her eyes filled with tears and she gave me an affectionate kiss, as she always did. In view of her condition, Helen and I stayed at a hotel.

We had to return home the next day, but I drove up the mountain and spent an hour with Judy before leaving. I asked if she had anything definite to discuss. In a weak voice whe replied, "No, Ike. I just wanted to see you once more. I feel much better for having seen you." I kissed her good-bye and she held my hand for a long time. She knew the end was near.

Judy died on Christmas Eve. Her condition had deteriorated rapidly and the last four weeks were spent in the hospital. For years she had sent us a lovely poinsettia every Christmas. During the day of December 24th the plant of the year before bloomed, and about 6:00 p.m. her new Christmas poinsettia arrived. Almost simultaneously the phone call came announcing her death. Needless to say, we had a sad Christmas.

Memorial services were held in Manchester the following week, and we drove up for the services, arriving the night before. Sybil had asked us to stay at the house. It was snowing hard when we arrived, and it snowed all night and the next morning. Since we were going down the mountain we managed to reach the church. But returning was different. Fortunately, roads had been plowed and cindered, but we had a real battle returning to the house.

I arranged to stay over a few days, as I wanted to take some preliminary steps in executing her estate. The will had to be probated thirty days before very much could be done. I found the Probate Judge, the Hon. Margaret Dougherty, to be very cooperative. After spending an hour with her, I rose to leave. Then she said, "Mr. Hoisington, your face is familiar and I think we have met before. Were you ever with Lionel D. Edie and Co.?" When I replied in the affirmative, she said, "I thought so. You replaced Dr. Shaw in 1942, and I was his secretary. I left when he did, so of course we didn't have a chance to get acquainted."

I wanted to go through Judy's safe and desks as soon as possible and remove all bank statements, tax returns and other important papers to Princeton. I asked Sybil to help me go through these papers the next day, and we worked from 9:00 a.m. to 4:00 p.m. Every single envelope had to be opened. In one, we found the missing 800 shares of Phillips Petroleum, some lovely jewelry, and a box of silver dollars, among other things. Naturally, all of these things had to be accounted for and became part of the estate.

Thirty days later I made an appointment in Philadelphia to open the safe deposit box. It is necessary on such occasions to have present a representative from the Internal Revenue Service, one from the State of Pennsylvania, and one from the bank. We were in for another surprise. We found a bundle of government bonds with uncut coupons ten years overdue. Judy had forgotten to tell me about them, and apparently had forgotten all about them herself.

By the spring of 1971, most of the important work in settling this estate had been finished, but we still had to hear from Internal Revenue on the federal tax return. My attorney tells me that this may happen in July, which means that it will have taken over five and one-half years to settle. The complexities and problems that arise in settling a sizable estate are amazing, and I believe they will become increasingly intricate as we go into the next decade.

Judy Babcock was a dear woman and we loved her as a valued friend and as a client. An ideal situation for an Investment Counselor would be to have twenty-five clients like Judy. I do have, and have had, several others like her, so I have been very fortunate.

PERLE FOLEY

I first met Perle Foley in the cocktail room at the Plaza. Jim Jackson, an old friend and business associate of her husband, who had recently died, introduced us. Jim and Perle's husband had been long-time friends in Texas and Kansas City, and she now turned to Jim for advice. He knew me well and had confidence in me, and so arranged our meeting.

Perle was then probably fifty-five. She was pretty, very petite, and always fashionably dressed. Like Sara Kent, she spoke with a lovely Southern accent. Her husband had had a prosperous cooperage business in Memphis, and they had kept a winter home in Sarasota, Florida. When he died suddenly, Perle was left a large sum of money.

Perle took Jim Jackson's advice and employed me that afternoon. The next day I met her to obtain a list of her securities, costs and other data, and we set up a custodian account with her broker so that sales and purchases could be made expeditiously. A few days later she left for her winter home, extending an invitation for Helen and me to visit her. We did so many times in Florida, and grew fonder of her with each visit. On our second visit Perle confided rather shyly, "Harland, I didn't reveal all of my assets to you when we met at the Plaza. I own quite a bit of real estate here in Florida." She had been quietly buying several pieces of land in Sarasota, which ultimately turned out to be very profitable investments.

As we developed our friendship with Perle we learned that she was an excellent bridge player as well as an expert at poker. In the early days of their marriage, her husband had run an extensive lumber operation in the Ozark Mountains of Missouri. It was necessary for them to live at the lumber camp several years. The evenings were long, and they spent many of them with the lumberjacks, playing poker.

Perle had been born in Poplar Bluff, Missouri, on October 23, 1880. Her parents were well-to-do and very puritanical. At an early age, Perle showed great ability as a pianist, and when she was thirteen years old, her teacher suggested she study under someone who could give her more advanced training. After two years of study at Hardin College in Mexico, Missouri, with an excellent German teacher who took only scholars with exceptional ability, she was advised to go to New York and study further with one of the prominent pianists of that time. Her father, however, said absolutely no – he would not have his daughter "go on the stage." Perle was heartbroken, but only briefly, for she met and fell in love with her future husband soon thereafter, married, and moved to his lumber camp in the Ozark Mountains.

Perle was dainty and rather frail. She eventually developed cancer and had to have most of her stomach removed. She made a good recovery and lived for several years after the operation. Like most of my women clients, she would not make a move of any importance without consulting me. Her operation was performed in New York and I went to see her one day when she was about ready to be discharged from the hospital. "Harland," she said, "my surgeon has advised me to go to Maine Chance for a month or two to recover. You know it costs a ghastly amount, and I want to know if you think I can afford it." Naturally I advised her to go; her income was sufficient and her health was important. She stayed for six weeks and felt much better, then went directly home to Sarasota. I made a brief visit there, as she wanted to change her will.

While there, I asked her one day just how expensive it had been at Maine Chance. She looked at me for a moment with her delightful, almost shy, expression and said, "Well, you know, Harland, most of the guests there were very wealthy women who spent their afternoons and evenings playing bridge. I was invited to play, but at first declined, saying that I didn't like to play for high stakes. But I watched carefully for three or four days and finally spotted a lady who was a real pro at bridge. I arranged to get her as a partner, and confidentially we 'went to town.' At one cent a point I won enough and more to pay all my expenses."

Perle was shy, coy, and innocent in appearance, but during the years spent in the lumber camp, she heard many spicy stories. Often she would suddenly tell one, and unless one knew her well, it would come as a real surprise. One of her choice stories went like this: Two sisters born into aristocracy of Back Bay Boston inherited quite a fortune. True to tradition, thrift and frugality had been greatly emphasized in their family. After the parents' death they lived together in a lovely area on Commonwealth Avenue, wore high laced shoes, and very tweedy suits. After some years, the younger sister finally tired of this rather dull existence and announced that she was leaving for New York to seek some gaiety. Her older sister was very much surprised, but finally consented on the condition that her sister would live on her income and never touch her principal.

For one whole year the younger sister stayed in New York. She rented a lovely apartment on 57th Street and wrote to her sister occasionally, but was really having herself a ball.

Eventually returning to Boston for a brief visit, she met her sister for lunch at the Copley Plaza. She was wearing a beautiful mink coat, a costly and fashionable suit and hat, and some newly acquired diamond rings. She looked like a model from Dior. Her older sister scarcely recognized her, and after a warm hug and kiss exclaimed, "My dear sister, have you been spending principal?" "No, my dear," was her response, "I have become a prostitute. It's a lovely occupation with plenty of income, and there is no sacrifice of principle."

Perle had one more story that I must relate. A very well-dressed, rather buxom middle-aged lady boarded a jet in London for New York. She was carrying Fifi, her little chihuahua. As she stepped into the plane the hostess smiled, "Madam, passengers cannot bring animals aboard the plane. You have time to go back to the desk, where they will be glad to place him in a nice little kennel and put him in the baggage compartment." The lady was downcast at the thought of her darling little Fifi traveling in such a dingy spot, but reluctantly turned back as though to follow instructions. As she retreated she had a happy thought. The dog was small, her bosom was ample; why not slip the dog into her blouse, button her coat and board the plane at the last minute? This she did. She took her seat next to a gentleman. Soon the plane taxied out for takeoff and she breathed a sigh of relief. As they became airborne the dog began struggling to get out. She folded her arms over her bosom, hoping to hide the commotion. It was obvious to the gentleman that something was wrong, but he elected to keep quiet. The dog continued to make frantic efforts to get out and there was such a commotion that the gentleman finally turned to the lady and said, "Madam, are you in trouble? Could I help you?" "No," she replied haughtily, "I am not in trouble." Finally the dog became so frantic that obviously something had to be done. The lady grimaced and was visibly in pain, so once again the gentleman asked, "May I assist you?" By this time the lady decided something had to be said; so she told the gentleman what had happened. "My God," he said, "Is the dog housebroken?" She replied, "Sir, that isn't the trouble. The problem is, he hasn't been weaned."

Perle's last illness came late in 1954. I learned from her daughter, Lois, who lived in Sarasota, that there was a recurrence of the cancerous condition. She continued to lose weight and it was obvious that she did not have long to live. Jim Jackson's daughter, Georgann, had married a very successful surgeon. He had a sanitarium at Croton-on-the-Hudson and Perle at last decided to go there for her final few months. She called me one day and asked if I would drive up from Princeton for a brief visit. It was a bitterly cold day in January. Helen went with me. The heater in our car failed to function and we were numb with cold on our arrival.

I was shocked at seeing Perle and knew that she was near death's door; her voice was so weak that it was difficult to understand her. She smiled, though, and finally said, "Harland, I have only a few days left. I know my will is in order because you just had it rewritten. You know that I am leaving most of my estate to Lois and that she is the executrix. I want to ask you to give Lois all the help you can in settling the estate. We both trust you implicitly." I assured her that I would.

Soon afterward, Perle expressed a desire to return to her Cunliff Lane home in Sarasota, and she was taken there by ambulance. Amazingly, she lived until summer, and died in her sleep one July night. Her passing brought great sorrow to me. Her courage, her sprightliness and her love of life had been a real inspiration.

I did go to Florida a few weeks later and gave Lois all the assistance I could in settling the estate. Lois was a sweet girl and for several years remained a client, prior to her death at rather an early age. In Sarasota she was widely known for her sweet disposition and for her genuine interest in animals as well as in people. A professional photographer, she could take you to Ringling Brothers winter headquarters and introduce you personally to all the animals.

THE TWO SISTERS FROM FORT WAYNE

ELOISE

My story would not be complete without a description of the McIntosh sisters from Fort Wayne, Indiana – Eloise and Beatrice. Their father had owned a large and very successful department store in Fort Wayne. Upon his death the sisters received not only many good securities from his estate, but also several thousand shares apiece of McIntosh Department Store stock. The company continued to prosper after his death, and paid nice dividends for many years.

I met Eloise, the older, first. She had married a fine young man from Cleveland who had died suddenly when about forty years of age. In addition to a lovely daughter, he had also left Eloise a handsome and rather sizable portfolio of securities.

Eloise came to New York, rented a nice apartment on lower Fifth Avenue, and sought advice from my firm. She had learned through mutual friends who were clients of mine in Cleveland that I was identified with Edie & Co., and asked that I be assigned to handle her account. She remained a client for about twenty-five years, during which time she never made a move of any importance without first seeking my advice.

New York was Eloise's home for three or four years. It was during her stay there that I established my own firm in Princeton. Loyally, Eloise stayed with me, as did most of my clients. In fact, by this time she vowed never to do business with anyone but me. I had her tax work done in Princeton, where she visited us several times a year. I saw that her will was rewritten, and that she utilized her maximum tax deductions by making gifts to her lovely daughter.

Eloise spent her summers near Manchester, Vermont. Finally, she decided to buy a spacious home in that area, but first I had to see it and decide if I thought she could afford it. I might add here that Eloise consistently ended each year in the red – in other words, she spent a little more than her income, and there was always the question of what securities to sell in order to pay taxes, my fee and other expenses.

When Eloise had become a client in 1942, we were up to our necks in World War II and stocks were greatly depressed. There was quite a sizable amount of life insurance money from her husband's estate and I used all of it to buy Standard Oil of New Jersey, General Motors, A.T. & T., Sears, Roebuck and other popular blue chips. The Dow-Jones Industrial Average was at about 150, so the portfolio fortunately experienced a fantastic increase in value over the years. Consequently, it was not difficult to raise a little extra money each year to meet the annual deficit.

Eloise had many charming qualities, but she also had some habits that were irritating. She would frequently call me at home on Saturday or Sunday to inquire about something trivial (i.e., she didn't quite understand her monthly statement) or some item that could have been discussed during the week. She might call about eleven o'clock Sunday night and say, "Ike, I can't understand this – my February income was only $2500 and I just can't see why the figure was so low." I would patiently explain as I had done on previous occasions that February and August were the two lowest months for income; that this would always hold, because for some reason dividends and interest seldom come due in those two months. "Oh," Eloise would say, "I remember now that you explained this before, and thank you very much. Good night."

As stated previously, I met with Eloise several times during the year. I would go over her portfolio slowly and carefully, discussing individual items. I would say, for instance, that her Amerada Petroleum that we purchased at $10 per share was now selling at 80; the A.T. & T. that we bought at $20 was now worth 50, Sears, Roebuck purchased at $10 was now 60, etc. I wanted her to know exactly what she owned, and also to realize that she was in a very fortunate position and that a good job had been done. I am sorry to say that the next day Eloise would have completely forgotten individual items as well as costs. To illustrate, A.T. & T. split three-for-one in 1959 and increased the dividend. This naturally was big news and highly publicized in the newspapers, on radio and television. Late on Saturday or Sunday Eloise called me and said, "Ike, I can't understand why I don't own A.T. & T. All of my friends own it and I think some of it should be in my portfolio." I replied, "Eloise, you do have 1,000 shares and your cost is $18 per share." I did not have her records at home, but an Investment Counselor somehow retains this kind of information. Eloise insisted, "I am sure you are mistaken." I replied that I would hold on while she obtained her latest appraisal. "Look under public utilities and you will find it." She soon returned and said, "You are absolutely right. I might have known that you would have A.T. & T. in my holdings and I apologize." This incident explains Eloise as best I can.

She remarried, in 1948, a very nice widower, Bill Armbruster. Eloise had known Bill and his wife, who were Manchester summer residents, very well. Since his work was in Philadelphia, they subsequently shared a lovely winter home in Philadelphia and the summer home in Manchester.

I grew to know Bill well and we were close friends. He never interfered with Eloise's financial affairs, realizing that he could not be helpful – and also that Eloise would not tolerate it. But I never saw him or talked with him during our fifteen years of friendship that he did not remark to me something to the effect of, "Ike, Eloise has unbounded confidence in you and I don't know to whom she would turn should you drop out of the picture."

Bill died suddenly in 1963 while Eloise was in London at the start of a world tour. Shortly after his death, she decided to rent an apartment on the Main Line. Bill had always paid her rent and bought the food, so he made quite a contribution to their overhead. When Eloise asked for my advice on the apartment I warned her that her living costs would now be much higher for two reasons. First, when married a joint return could be filed, but as a widow her income tax would be much higher; and second, Bill had paid the rent and the grocery bills. I doubted that she could afford the apartment and the expensive summer home in Manchester. My advice was to spend eight months in Manchester and to go to Florida for three or four months. I could see that she had her heart set on the apartment, however, and she called me one day to say that she had rented it for only $500 a month. I knew then that she was in trouble, but it would have been useless to oppose her.

Because of Bill's death and because of the approximately $10,000-a-year increase in overhead, Eloise began to get irritable and critical. I took it for a year but in 1965 I wrote her a nice letter saying I thought it would be better if she went somewhere else for advice, and offered to help her find a satisfactory Investment Counselor. She received my letter on a Saturday morning. That night, true to form, she called me at home about 11:00 p.m. and was hysterical. How could I be so callous after all these years? She would lose her mind if I did not consent to continue with her. I placated her as best I could and after half an hour agreed to reconsider, providing she changed her habits. I did continue for another year, reluctantly, when out of the blue I received a letter saying that she had decided to switch over to a well-known Investment Counsel firm. I think her son-in-law, a fine gentleman, had influenced her to do this. I was greatly relieved and wrote her a very nice good-bye letter, wishing her the best of luck. . . .

BEATRICE

Eloise was a very attractive woman with impeccable taste in dress and in furnishing her home. Her sister, Beatrice, however, I think surpassed her a little in each of these two categories. Beatrice was more careful of her budget and didn't spend much more than her income would permit. She had a good business head and I often thought that she should have remained in Fort Wayne and been an executive in the family's department store.

I first met Beatrice in Cleveland. Eloise had kept her Cleveland house for about a year before selling it. There was a family reunion, and I was invited to attend. More than anything else Eloise wanted Beatrice's husband to "pass" on me and to be assured that she was in the hands of a competent man who would not make passes at a pretty young widow. Beatrice had married a very attractive and successful man from Knoxville, Tennessee. I thought he was tops, and went back to New York hoping I had successfully passed inspection.

In 1947 Eloise called me from Manchester to say that Beatrice was there from Knoxville, with her two children, and was anxious to see me on a very confidential matter. Could I drive up the next day? Of course, I said I could, and arrived the following day without any idea of what we were to discuss. To make a long story short, Beatrice informed me that she was flying to Reno the next day to file for a divorce from her husband, Edward. She had left Knoxville with her two children, leaving Edward with the impression that she would be visiting Eloise for a week or two. Developments would come as a complete surprise to him.

She further informed me that she had had to depart hurriedly, leaving all of her personal securities and most of her jewelry in her safe deposit box in Knoxville. She wanted to employ me as her Investment Counselor. My first task would be to fly there, obtain the items, and bring them back to Princeton. I would take a letter to the president of the bank authorizing me to have access to the box and to take possession of the securities and jewelry. I agreed to undertake the mission the following day.

Edward knew me from previous meetings, so I needed to get into and out of the bank as quickly as possible. Her husband being a bank director, Beatrice was afraid he might see me and that my presence in Knoxville would arouse his suspicions.

With all credentials intact, I flew to Knoxville the following day out of Philadelphia. I arrived there about midnight on one of the hottest July nights I have ever experienced. To complicate matters the airline did not deplane my suitcase, which went on to Oklahoma City. The officials assured me that it would be returned to my hotel by 8:00 a.m. the next morning. I never did get the bag. The hotel had no air conditioning and I spent a restless and miserable night, awakening finally to find that my bag was still missing and that the stores did not open until 10:00 a.m.; I needed fresh underclothing and a new shirt. I also had to go to a barber shop for a shave. My appointment at the bank was at ten, and in my rush to get there, I let a taxi driver slam the door on my thumb and it was really smashed. I arrived at the bank rather weak and with my handkerchief wrapped around a thumb bleeding profusely. Fortunately, they had a first aid department and a nurse who shortly had me properly repaired.

The president of the bank was very cooperative. He assigned his secretary to assist me in making an inventory of the securities. I forget how many stock certificates there were, but in any case we began about 11:00 a.m. and did not finish until 4:00, with a few minutes out for a sandwich. The young lady was very helpful, and placed all the securities in a large manila envelope addressed to me in Princeton. We took them to the post office, insured them, and obtained the necessary receipts. I breathed a sigh of relief. I still had a large package of expensive jewelry, but elected to carry it back to Princeton with me. My return flight left Knoxville at 6:00 p.m., so I hurried to the airport. My plane arrived, and while I stood at the gate watching the arriving passengers, who appeared but the husband, Edward. Fortunately, he did not see me, and I never knew where he had come from. Naturally, I never made any inquiries.

Arriving back in Princeton, I established a custodian account for Beatrice at a local bank, made a new appraisal of the securities, and found that I had a very sizable new advisory account. I called Beatrice in Reno to tell her I had successfully made the journey to Knoxville, and that the securities and jewelry were all safe in Princeton. Naturally, she was relieved and grateful.

She added that she had also left her Cadillac in Knoxville and would like it in Reno. Could I solve this little problem? I said that our youngest son, Dick, was in school at Vanderbilt, in Nashville, and that I would call and ask him if he could drive the car to Reno. This was right up Dick's alley and all arrangements were made. He received the key from Beatrice with instructions to the garage in Knoxville, and left early Tuesday. I didn't realize it at the time, but he wanted to be back in Birmingham on Saturday, as the annual football game between Alabama and Vanderbilt was scheduled that day. This was a real must, so Dick had Tuesday, Wednesday, Thursday and Friday to reach Reno, and return. Reach it he did, delivered the car to Beatrice, and caught a plane in the same breath for Birmingham. I learned later that he had to go to San Francisco to get a plane for New Orleans and thence to Birmingham. He arrived Saturday just in time for the kickoff.

Beatrice's stay in Reno, I believe, was about two months. She was in constant touch with me by phone or letter. At the end of the first month she called to say that when her divorce became final she had decided to come east with the children and stay in Princeton temporarily. It would give us a chance to go over her investments thoroughly, and in the meantime could I do her a few favors, such as: 1. Secure suitable living quarters for her and the children. Something very nice but inexpensive. 2. Secure a good lawyer – she wanted an excellent lawyer, but at a reasonable price. 3. Would I consider going on the department store's Board in Fort Wayne to represent her interest and Eloise's? I would, of course, receive a small director's fee and would have to go to Fort Wayne four times a year. 4. Finally, would I find a capable babysitter – at a reasonable price – as she did not wish to be tied down too closely?

Again I want to emphasize that Beatrice was a very attractive girl and that she dressed beautifully. She finally arrived in Princeton with her young son and daughter. We met her at the station with our station wagon, knowing there would be large amounts of luggage, drove her to the hotel (which was fairly reasonable), helped her get settled, and bade her good night. She appeared at the office the next morning saying that her quarters were not what she wanted. Could I secure better ones? I recommended an inn that was more luxurious and consequently more expensive.

Beatrice was in the office each day for the first two weeks. We did have quite a few changes to make in the portfolio, but these were all consummated to her satisfaction. Did I know a good golf course where I could get her a guest card? I knew one and obtained the guest card; then we loaned her one of our cars, for she had sold her Cadillac in Reno.

Quite soon, and not to our surprise, a handsome young man from New York – a previous acquaintance – began to appear each weekend. Many times Helen kept the children while Beatrice played golf or went to the shore with John. Finally, she tired of the inn and rented a furnished house in a lovely section of Princeton. Again we loaned her our station wagon to move and get settled. She found a maid and we were relieved of babysitting.

Within a year Beatrice and John were married and they rented a lovely apartment on Park Avenue. As the children matured (and they were lovely children; the girl was strikingly beautiful), they were instructed by Beatrice to always go to "Uncle Ike" should any emergency arise. The family came to Princeton occasionally as our weekend guests and on some weekends, when we were away, we gave them a key to the house in our absence.

As time went on I did agree to go to Fort Wayne frequently to the directors' meetings. I soon realized that the "men in charge" would not welcome me on the Board, but it was perfectly agreeable for me to attend the meetings. The trip overnight on the train was not too pleasant.

Beatrice, as I have said, was a good businesswoman, careful with money, and very imaginative. The income from her securities, while very sizable, was never quite enough. Consequently, she was looking for ways of increasing it. The store in Fort Wayne bought all merchandise through a cartel in New York. Beatrice, as well as all stockholders, could get merchandise through this cartel, or buying agent, at a big discount. So it appeared that orders for mink coats might prove lucrative, and when Beatrice informed me of this I sent several of my clients to buy mink coats from her. What the amount of money totaled I never knew, but I suspect it was substantial.

I advised many of my clients to leave their securities with good brokerage firms who were members of the New York Stock Exchange. There was no charge providing all trading was done through them. Clients received monthly statements itemizing their securities and income, and were sent a check each month for income collected. In addition, duplicate confirmations were sent to me so that my records were always up to date. It was convenient for income tax records, and there was no custodian fee, so all in all it worked out very nicely.

About 1965 or 1966, some friend convinced Beatrice that keeping her securities with a broker was unsafe. Try as I might, I could not convince her that her friend was wrong. Finally I stopped trying, and she made arrangements to open a custodian account with a bank. Charges for this service were quite sizable, and Beatrice determined that she could not afford the custodian fee as well as mine. As a matter of fact, she had such huge profits in most of her securities that it was difficult to make changes. Beatrice realized this, and also that her securities were all of the blue chip variety; therefore, she could dismiss me and save my fee. I could see through her reasoning and consequently made no attempt to keep her as a client. So we had a very pleasant parting after twenty years of association and as far as I know she is now living happily somewhere in Westchester County, New York.

This ends my story of the two sisters from Fort Wayne. They were attractive, challenging in different ways, and for the most part interesting clients. Certainly, with them, there were very few dull moments.

LUCY DiFLAVIANO COOPER

After W.W. I., in Altoona, Pennsylvania, Mrs. Dorinda DiFlaviano presented her husband, Amadeo, with a lovely girl, Lucia. At the time there were two other children, and two more would follow, so that the DiFlavianos eventually had three girls and two boys.

Amadeo had emigrated from Italy at the age of sixteen; Dorinda followed when she was twenty-one, and they were married. In the 1890's, the United States was in the throes of a depression, with unemployment high. But Amadeo was willing to turn his hand to anything that would produce income, and secured work with the Pennsylvania Railroad at Altoona.

The first few years were difficult ones. Frugality and hard work were emphasized in the DiFlaviano household. All of the children learned to work at an early age, and contributed as much as possible to providing for the necessities of life.

Dorinda and Amadeo had no inkling that Lucy would some day become a very successful businesswoman as well as a fine homemaker and mother. "Precocious" is the best word to describe her. From the day she entered first grade, it was evident that she was not only brilliant but ambitious. By sacrificing, her parents were able to see her through high school, but there were no funds for college. In any case, Lucy felt that she should begin helping the rest of the family financially.

Although adept at typing and shorthand, she found no work – of any kind – available in Altoona. Finally, she learned of a job opening with the Pennsylvania Highway Department in Hollidaysburg, twenty-five miles from Altoona. The salary was twenty-five dollars a week. Lucy took it, and for two years drove fifty miles a day in order to bring in this income.

These were the days of the New Deal and the Depression. Our government was adding many people to the payrolls to staff the numerous agencies being created. In 1939, Lucy went to Washington to seek better employment, and her abilities were instantly recognized. She was given a promising assignment as a trainee job analyst with the General Accounting Office. During her tenure with the government, she traveled for more than five years throughout the United States and rose to the head of her organization, eventually becoming chief job analyst in the Washington Bureau, Department of the Army. Subsequently, she worked on a consulting basis with the United Nations Secretariat in setting up job analysis programs, and received the Meritorious Award, one of the highest civilian awards, for exceptional contribution in this area.

Finally, when she was about twenty-eight, Lucy met the man she had been hoping to find. Guy D. Cooper was stationed in Washington in the Army as an expert on transportation. Previously, he had been a corporate officer with Cooper-Jarrett, Inc., a highly successful trucking company with headquarters in Chicago. A year and a half later, in 1946, they were married, and when the war ended took up their residence in Naperville, a lovely suburb west of Chicago. There, after her marriage, Lucy performed management studies for several private concerns and wrote free-lance articles for trade journals.

In time, Guy was made President of Cooper-Jarrett. In 1961, they were living happily in Naperville with their young son, Robert, when Guy and Lucy made a routine business trip to Washington. While making a telephone call from their hotel suite there, Guy died suddenly and without warning.

I attended the funeral in Naperville, and Lucy asked me the

following morning if I would consent to continue on as her Investment Counselor. Naturally, I agreed. To my horror, she told me that Guy had died "intestate." This complicates matters in any state, but in Illinois the complications were nearly overwhelming. In the estate were the lovely home in Naperville, a large ranch in Mississippi (unfortunately jointly-owned with a neighbor), some life insurance monies, and common stock of a considerable amount. Fortunately, Lucy was able to secure the highly professional services of Judge Mel Abrahamson, a family friend, to start the wheels in motion in settling the estate. But it took almost four years to finally accomplish it.

In the meantime, Lucy decided to trade country living and horses for a new life with her son, Robert, in the South. Moving to Fort Lauderdale, she became an analytical writer for a prominent agricultural firm. Her work took her on frequent trips throughout the Caribbean and the major agricultural areas of the United States.

In time, Lucy felt this much traveling took her away from her teenage son too much, so she moved from analytical writing for a single company into the area of free-lance writing for several. One of her most fascinating assignments in recent months has been writing columns for the Fort Lauderdale weekly newspaper and feature articles for a popular Southern Florida magazine, *Pictorial Life.* But throughout it all, and in whatever she undertakes, she has never lost that spirit of youthful enthusiasm and drive nor the quiet but determined thoroughness in her approach to obstacles that so characterized her early years.

Lucy is petite in form, modest, and beautiful. Dark-eyed and with coal-black hair, she typifies the beauty of Italian women. Needless to say, she has been a wonderful client – completely cooperative, gracious and complimentary. Needless to say, *Io l'adoro.*

PART FOUR

1950-1960

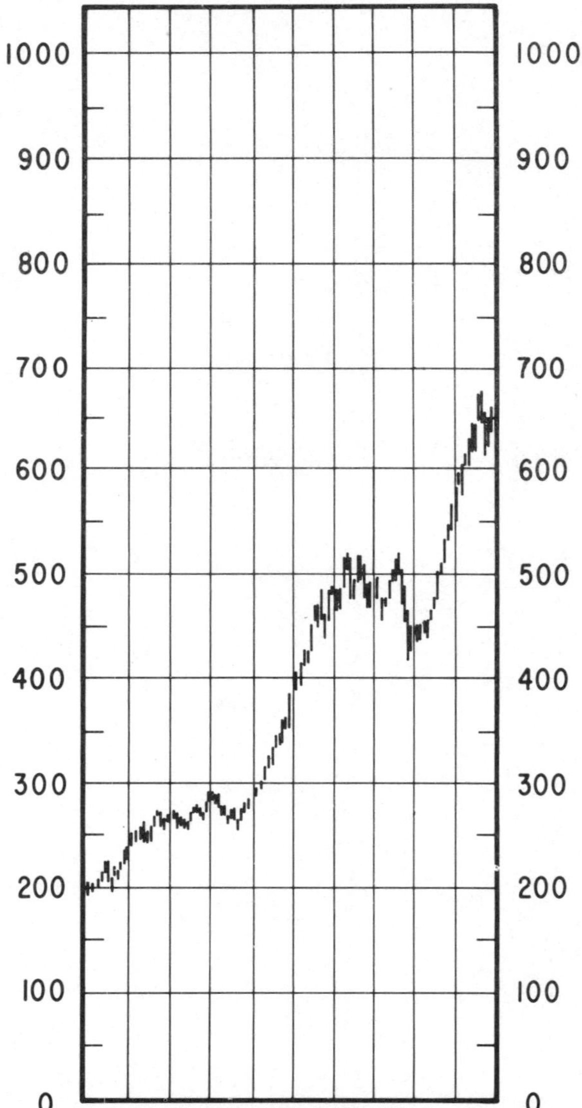
1000
900
800
700
600
500
400
300
200
100
0
1950
51
52
53
54
55
56
57
58
59

CHAPTER ONE

THE DECADE IN PREVIEW

As we entered 1950, there were few indications that we were soon to emerge into the greatest two decades of prosperity this nation or any nation had ever experienced. As the chart opening this decade shows, in 1950 the Dow-Jones Industrial Average was still below the high point of 294.07 reached in 1930. In 1951-1952-1953, the rise was gradual, with the Average finally exceeding this 1930 high in 1954. From this point on, it climbed at a rapid rate and in 1959 reached a new high of 679.36. We had entered the greatest bull market of all time, that was to reach its peak in the following decade – 995 in 1966.

In 1950, Harry S. Truman was in the fifth year of his Presidency. He had facilitated some constructive developments. The Marshall Plan, European Recovery Act, and NATO had all given the world new confidence. The cold war with Russia was still with us and the Berlin situation tense and disturbing;but on the whole, it seemed that we had reason to hope for a peaceful and productive period ahead.

These hopes were soon shattered. On a lovely Sunday morning, June 25, 1950, we were startled to learn that South Korea had been invaded by North Korean Communists. Without hesitation, President Truman declared our determination to resist this aggressive act under the aegis of the United Nations, and sent American troops to Korea. General Douglas MacArthur assumed command, by appointment, of the United Nations military forces in South Korea. Out of the blue, we were suddenly engaged in a bloody "police action" in Asia, to experience great loss of life on both sides.

Naturally, markets were nervous, and a fairly sharp decline occurred in the weeks following the news of South Korea's invasion. One or two of my clients became so frightened that they asked me to sell all of their common stocks. I refused, pointing out that not only would they incur large capital gains, but they also might lose their position through failure to repurchase at the right time.

On July 5, 1950, I sent the following policy letter to my clients:

"Quite obviously the stock market is in a highly emotional condition, and for a period of time will be mostly a reflection of spot news developments. In addition, the circulation of an increasing number of rumors and half-truths is to be expected. These factors in combination with the magnitude of the drop create a situation where short, sharp moves are to be expected at any time. However, unless the Korean situation takes an unexpected turn for the better, we are likely to see a further decline in the market. The magnitude of the effort to be required of us in Korea seems to be increasing, and certainly the possibility of further adverse news is a very real one.

"If a long war can be avoided, the market will again give greater consideration to the trend of earnings, yields, and tangible assets, plus the definite prospects of increased armament expenditures, which appear inevitable regardless of the outcome of the Korean War. There is no doubt that confidence, which is so essential to a strong market, has received a severe shock, but eventually the trend of events may prove that current pessimism has been carried too far. The contingency of war must be given careful consideration in current investment policies.

"At the moment, I advise against indiscriminate buying or selling of common stocks, but do suggest a review of holdings to determine what action may be required to reduce disproportionate risks through inadequate diversification by industry, or by undue geographical concentration of assets, or vulnerability to imposition of wartime controls . . . ."

The intervention of the Chinese Communists in Korea late in November, 1950, changed the course of the war and caused the U. N. forces to retreat south of the 38th parallel. General MacArthur favored bombing the Chinese Communists, maintaining privileged sanctuary in Manchuria, blockading the Chinese coast, and utilizing the Chinese Nationalist forces of General Chiang Kai-shek. Truman opposed this largely because of opposition by the United Nations. MacArthur felt that since the U. S. was bearing 90% of the burden, we should disregard the U. N.'s wishes and pursue military expediency.

When the distinguished soldier and statesman was relieved of his duties in Korea in December, 1950 by President Truman, it created quite an uproar. Naturally, there were some who agreed with Truman, but millions of Americans felt that MacArthur's position was justified. MacArthur had never liked Truman and did not conceal his feelings, so there was a definite clash of personalities.

MacArthur's previous accomplishments and honors had been many and varied. Among other things, he graduated first in his class in 1903 from West Point, and was advanced to Brigadier General in the First World War. Made a Major General in 1925, he was the youngest of that rank in the Army. He was appointed U. S. Chief of Staff with rank as full General by President Hoover in November, 1930, commanding the Department of the Philippines. In October, 1935, he retired as Chief of Staff to become Military Adviser to the Philippine Government. After the Philippine Army was reincorporated into U. S. forces in July, 1941, President Franklin D. Roosevelt made him Lieutenant General in command of U. S. and Commonwealth forces in the Philippines. He was renamed full General by Roosevelt.

MacArthur's courageous fight when greatly outnumbered by Japanese forces on the Bataan peninsula will long be remembered. He escaped by plane with some of his leaders, flying to Australia. Subsequently, the job of gradually subduing the Japanese forces and then recapturing the Philippines was skillfully accomplished. After World War II, President Truman appointed him Supreme Commander of the Allied Forces in Japan and for five years he supervised this country's reconstruction and democratization.

A proud and vain man, MacArthur deeply resented his dismissal from Korea. On his return to America, he was honored by being asked to address a joint session of Congress. His address was touching, eloquent, and brilliant; its closing words will be long remembered: "Old soldiers never die, they just fade away."

Truman declined renomination in 1952, and the Democratic Party nominated Adlai Stevenson to oppose General Dwight D. Eisenhower. But Eisenhower won an overwhelming victory, and assumed office on January 20, 1953. He had promised to go to Korea, if elected, and end the war. He carried out this promise, but hostilities did not actually cease until July 27, 1953.

In 1954 the excess profits tax was repealed and we were again on a peacetime footing. The market started to move up and reached 404.39, its highest level since April, 1930. From this point on for the remainder of the decade, the market enjoyed a steady and very substantial rise. There were some investors who had sold fearfully at the outbreak of the Korean hostilities, and they never reestablished their positions.

Eisenhower was a President who enjoyed the nation's confidence and respect, and who followed a middle-of-the-road policy in domestic decisions. He submitted, and Congress approved, some of the highest peacetime budgets in history. However, in 1954 he had Congress pass a substantial tax cut, and with it an overall revision of the whole tax structure. During this year he also had a successful and highly publicized confrontation with Senator Joseph McCarthy.

Joseph Raymond McCarthy was elected U. S. Senator from

Wisconsin in 1946, having defeated Senator Robert M. La Fallette, Jr. for the Republican Senatorial nomination, and going on to win over the Democratic nominee by a wide margin. Senator McCarthy received national attention in February, 1950 in a speech made at Wheeling, West Virginia. In it, he claimed that our State Department was infiltrated with Communists. He charged many other prominent officials with Communist tendencies. In many cases, he seemed to have evidence to back up his charges, but his methods were widely disputed and his reputation for veracity gradually diminished.

In December, 1954, the Senate, acting on a motion of censure against him, voted to condemn McCarthy for contempt of a Senate Elections Subcomittee that had investigated his conduct and financial affairs in 1952; for abuse of certain Senators; and for insults to the Senate itself during the censure proceedings. With this rebuke, McCarthy's influence in the Senate steadily diminished until his death in 1957. But the entire affair had roused national feelings to the boiling point – depending on which side of the argument one's sentiments lay.

In 1954, the Supreme Court made one of the most important decisions of the twentieth century regarding civil rights, declaring racial segregation in public schools unconstitutional; in 1955 it banned segregation in publicly financed parks, playgrounds, and golf courses. Subsequent action by the Court and the Interstate Commerce Commission barred segregation in public transportation.

Naturally, there were many who criticized the Supreme Court for these decisions, but on the other hand, there were millions of Americans who applauded them. At long last the American Negro was given rights that should have been extended to him years before. From this point on, the Negro would gradually be released from servitude and given an opportunity to be on equal grounds, under law, with other citizens. As one authority stated, "Today in the black community, the impossible dream of freedom, dignity, and education is finally, but slowly, becoming a reality."

As we entered 1955, President Eisenhower's popularity with the people grew. The nation's sense of confidence was reflected in a buoyant stock market, which approached the 500 level. In September of this year, Eisenhower was vacationing in Colorado, and while trout fishing at a high altitude, he suffered a severe coronary thrombosis. The market dropped sharply. Nothing will disturb it more than uncertainty. But the President made a good recovery – as did the market – and in 1956 he was reelected over Adlai Stevenson by an even wider margin than in 1952.

At the beginning of his second term, he advocated the so-called "Eisenhower Doctrine," in which he proposed to send military and economic assistance to any Middle Eastern nation requesting it. This doctrine was designed to bolster these countries against Communist aggression, and under its terms the U. S. Marines were sent to Lebanon in July, 1958. A year earlier, the President had sent Federal troops to enforce a court-ordered integration decision in Little Rock, Arkansas. These events, with others, served to increase the nation's confidence in the man and his leadership, and the market continued strong – reaching a peak of 588 in 1958.

During the 1957-1958 period, inflationary momentum persisted and increased. Fear of inflation undoubtedly influenced the policy of many investors, causing them to seek capital gains by means of the equity market.

A sharp business recession in 1958 caused a slump in the upward march of security prices, but by 1959 the economy had recovered and the Dow-Jones Industrial Average touched a new high of 679.36.

The buoyant quality of the stock market during this decade closely parallels the psychological mood of the nation, which remained relaxed and optimistic for the most part. Although it is difficult to measure, this mood was influenced to a great extent by the tremendous confidence people had in Eisenhower and in his leadership qualities. Although uttered ten years later, upon Eisenhower's death on March 28, 1969, CBS News Correspondent Eric Sevareid's comments convey the magnetic quality of our thirty-fourth President as well as the regard in which he was held by his countrymen:

"He was a man for all seasons. If it can be said that a mass of people can love a single person, this man was so loved. He was homespun and prosaic, his speech was simple and stumbling – and he was larger than life.

"He could not lose. He could do no wrong. He was the son every old man wanted, the father every child wanted, and brother for everyone else. He was the whole man, the total personality.

"People like this man for two reasons as old as man's time on earth – because they trusted him and because he made them feel good.

"He was a Republican and Democrats felt a glow in his presence; he was the big brass and common soldiers found him their kind of guy.

"He was the victorious Commander-in-Chief of the greatest armies ever assembled, but he would have felt silly on a white horse.

"His magic secret was his incandescent charm. But on what pedestal will his place in history really rest?

"Not on his work as Chief of Staff of the post-war army, where he left no particular imprint. Not on his work as the head of Columbia University, where he was singularly out of place and even his presidency will be much disputed, for he did not really enjoy the exercise of power and he took the country on no bold new courses; rather, he presided, calmly, over a generally calm period and allowed the people to think of other things, unworried. He gave his country the respite it badly needed.

"His real works in life were two: first, the prosecution of the great war in North Africa and Europe, where he was not a fighting soldier like a Patton, not a strategist like MacArthur, nor an administrator like General Marshall – but a superb coordinator who induced strong men of many services and many nations to work together. Such was his magical quality that all men wished to please him, even the Titan Churchill.

"Second, the breathing of life into the North Atlantic Military Alliance when again he traveled Europe, urging, charming, persuading the governments living under the deepening shadow of Russian power to again plan and work together, and the European peace he had done so much to win, *was* reinsured, and *was* kept – to this day.

"Mr. Eisenhower thought of himself as a man of the old school, and he was truly a *man* in the meaning of the familiar poem by the poet of the old school, Kipling.

"Dwight Eisenhower *did* talk with crowds but kept his virtue. He *did* walk with kings nor lost the common touch."[1]

1. Used by permission of Eric Sevareid

CHAPTER TWO

ELECTRONICS

"Electronics" has been described as "the study of the properties and behavior of electrons under all conditions, especially with reference to technical and industrial applications."

Early in the 1950's a wave of small and large electronic firms mushroomed. Growth of television, the transistor radio, computers, space study, aviation – all brought about the transistor, the diode, the integrated circuit.

As electronics companies all over the nation sprang into being, investors demanded that a portion of their funds be placed in these stocks. Some large companies, such as Texas Instruments, Hewlett Packard, Varian Associates, Hughes Aircraft, Thompson-Ramo-Wooldridge and Sylvania prospered and have grown into large and, on the whole, successful companies. Investors who bought into them in the early stages have done extremely well. But on the opposite side, literally thousands of smaller companies were organized, and capital raised through the sale of common stock. Investors went after the stock as though any company in the electronic world would make them rich overnight. Stocks offered at $2 per share would be selling at 20 within three or four months, despite the fact that earnings – or any sound indication of future earnings – were totally lacking. Statistics are not available, but it is safe to say that 80% to 90% of these small companies failed, with investors losing everything. Failures were generally the result of poor management combined with overly optimistic – and sometimes grandiose – expectations.

Princeton did not escape these developments. Because Princeton University had an excellent Engineering School, many talented scientists were in the area. The Forrestal Laboratory and other important scientific projects also attracted them.

It would be impossible to say, but I know of at least ten small electronics companies that were formed in Princeton. In most cases, management rested with talented scientists who commanded great respect. At least 80% of these firms failed, but not before the stocks had skyrocketed to fantastic figures.

I remember one company very well. Stock was offered at around $2 and went as high as 25. It was actively traded. In the first year, earnings were so sparse that one couldn't see them with a microscope. Several of my clients insisted on buying this stock and to oppose them would have been sheer folly.

One day I made an appointment to meet the president. He was a charming man and a truly gifted scientist. It didn't take me more than an hour to realize that he was also an idealist with absolutely no business ability. I returned to my office and convinced my clients that the stock should be sold. It was then at 21. It is now about 1; the company is still breathing, but not too audibly.

These preliminary remarks on electronics, however, lead me to a more interesting story – the more so because one of the two organizers was a good client of mine.

This gentleman interested a very able man in Princeton to join forces with him. Neither could be called a scientist, but both were stable men who surrounded themselves with good minds.

The company was launched with great fanfare. In no time at all the public (mostly Princetonians) gobbled up 800,000 shares of the million-share offering, with the balance being retained by the founders. The offering price was low – two or three dollars a share. Soon it was selling at 12, then 14, 18, and eventually 25 and 30.

After a year (no earnings yet) a New York firm called me to say that they had a client who wanted to buy 10,000 shares at 14. Could I uncover that much stock? I said I would try.

I went to my client and persuaded him to let 10,000 go at 14. He was very reluctant to sell. Soon it was 16 and another bid came for 10,000 at 16. Again, my client was extremely reluctant, but I pointed out that he would still have 80,000 shares. He finally agreed. At 18 we sold another 10,000, and at 20 another 10,000 shares.

Eventually the company went into bankruptcy, and today the stock can be used as a wall decoration. My client died within two years. His lovely wife is still a client, and one of the nicest anyone could have. She has since remarried and moved to the West. Helen and I visit her frequently and these visits are always a great treat.

If statistics were available on the amount of money lost on investments in small electronics companies during the Fifties, I am sure they would be too astronomical to be believed.

CHAPTER THREE

WILKES-BARRE

This city of about 80,000, county seat of Luzerne County, Pennsylvania, contains some of the warmest, finest people I have met during my counseling years. Since 1942 I have been a regular visitor to Wilkes-Barre at least once a month, which has meant twelve trips for twenty-seven years – or a total of about 324 visits. I regard it as my second home, and have often thought of moving there.

Anthracite coal, discovered about 1870, was responsible for much of the wealth in Wilkes-Barre. The Wyoming Valley and the mountains on either side of the Susquehanna River had tremendous deposits of the Black Gold – sometimes referred to as "Black Diamonds."

Soon after joining Lionel D. Edie & Company, I met a Mr. John H. Blackman, who came into our New York office seeking Investment Counsel service for a sizable church fund. "Jack" was a member of the church and Chairman of the Finance Committee, as well as the principal agent for Mutual Life Insurance Company of New York in Northeastern Pennsylvania. His closest friend in their New York office was a man named Oliver Whipple, who had long been a good friend of mine; therefore Jack was advised to ask for me. I might add that this was one of the luckiest breaks I've had.

After a brief chat, Jack invited me to come to Wilkes-Barre to discuss our proposals with the Finance Committee. I went the next week, met the Committee, and it was agreed that they would employ Lionel D. Edie & Company. Apparently we pleased Jack Blackman, for beginning in 1942, he and others began recommending me to a number of people; eventually, when I had gone into business for myself in Princeton, I had about twenty-five clients in Wilkes-Barre.

Jack was a director of one of the largest banks in Wilkes-Barre. Several key men had gone into the Armed Services, the president of many years had just died, and the bank suddenly found itself very short-handed. The trust officer had assumed the duties of the president's office as well as the responsibilities of a large Trust Department. Jack came to me one day and asked whether I would be interested in taking over, with the assistance of the Trust Committee, the responsibility of managing the bank's various trusts. There were about seventy, some of them quite sizable. I asked about the mechanics and what would be expected of me, and learned that my duties would include the holding of monthly meetings with the Trust Committee, preparation of all appraisals, and the supervision of each trust. The undertaking would be quite time-consuming and entail a tremendous amount of responsibility. After consulting my associates, I accepted the assignment.

I think I can say that this was one of the most rewarding and challenging jobs I ever undertook. For over fifteen years I made virtually all the decisions and recommendations for every trust in the bank. The Committee was most cooperative. I was bullish on the market and stocks were very cheap when I first started, so results were fantastically good. In addition, I formed a "Common Trust Fund" and a "Legal Trust Fund," and had the responsibility of managing these monies. At long last the bank grew to the point where it needed its own Investment Department, and so my services were no longer needed. I was not disappointed, for I had recently lost one of my key men in Princeton, and the fee from the bank was no longer commensurate with the work involved. But I relinquished the assignment with the feeling that a splendid job had been done. I still receive warm acknowledgments from, and stay in touch with, many of the individuals whose trusts I managed those many years.

F. M. Kirby & Company was a five-and-dime store which later formed the nucleus of the great F. W. Woolworth enterprise, for it was F. M. Kirby who was a co-founder of this international business. The company joined Woolworth in 1912, but today Woolworth's store in Wilkes-Barre has this sign above the entance:

F. W. WOOLWORTH & CO.
successors to
F. M. KIRBY & CO.

Wilkes-Barre is really the home of the five-and-ten-cent store, and there's a reason, dating back to these days early in the century, that Woolworth store fronts are painted in red. Fred Morgan Kirby, American merchant and banker, was born in Brownsville, New York, in 1861. In 1884 he moved to Wilkes-Barre, and opened his first five-and-ten-cent store under the name of Woolworth & Kirby. By 1887, he had acquired C. S. Woolworth's share in the store, reorganizing it as F. M. & W. Kirby, the "W." standing for William, his father.

In 1912 Mr. Kirby was operating ninety-six stores east of the Mississippi River, and it was in this year that he joined forces with the F. W. Woolworth Company, becoming president. His life was one of unceasing philanthropy and he eventually became one of the world's wealthiest men. His benefactions to Wilkes-Barre exceeded many millions of dollars, and upon his passing, his son, Allan P. Kirby, continued in his footsteps.

F. M. Kirby decided to sell his Watertown, New York, store and bring the merchandise and store manager, Frederick J. Weckesser, to Wilkes-Barre. Rather than move the entire inventory, they decided to sell as much of it as possible in Watertown. Consequently, two huge tables were placed in front of the store windows and were covered with a bright red cloth. All merchandise was marked at either five cents or ten cents, and was quickly liquidated. There must have been the feeling that the bright red colors stimulated sales; at least, it was adopted as the color for all Woolworth's stores, a tradition that still prevails in many parts of the country.

In 1912, when the Kirby stores merged with Woolworth, Frederick Weckesser from the Watertown store became district manager as well as member of the Woolworth Board of Directors and a leading figure in the Executive Committee. His beautiful mansion, located at 170 S. Franklin Street, was later given to Wilkes College; today, Weckesser Hall embraces the offices of the President of the College and other administrative offices. It goes without saying that the Kirbys, Weckessers and several other Wilkes-Barre residents became owners of substantial amounts of Woolworth stock, and consequently enormously wealthy.

It would require more words than space and time allow to write about all the wonderful people I have met and served in this fine city. Not all of them are clients; some are or have been. In addition to the following two, who are not described in any particular order, I came to know and respect many other prominent citizens.

GILBERT S. McCLINTOCK

1890 – 1962

Gilbert McClintock was an eminent attorney and patron of the arts who served as a Trustee of Princeton University, President and a

Director of the Glen Alden Coal Company, Chairman of the Board of the Miners National Bank, and Chairman of the Board of Trustees of Wilkes College. The following excerpt appeared in *Wilkes College Campus, 1968,* depicting the Wilkes-Barre residence McClintock bequeathed to Wilkes College upon his death:

"McClintock Hall, 44 South River Street, was a gift to the College in 1951 of the late Attorney Gilbert S. McClintock when he served as the Chairman of the Board of Trustees of the College. Erected originally in 1841, it is now used as a girl's dormitory.

"Attorney McClintock was a staunch friend and advisor of the College. He was foremost among those of his era in his civic work and leadership. Indeed, during the latter years of his life he was known as 'Mr. Wilkes-Barre' and his intimates respected him as such.

"He was the son of Attorney Andrew Hamilton McClintock and the great, great grandson of Charles Cist, an 18th century publisher associated with Benjamin Franklin. Among the books Cist published were two by Thomas Paine.

"Although his forebears settled in Northumberland County in 1795, Attorney McClintock was born in Wilkes-Barre where he lived his life. He was educated at Princeton University and received his law degree from the University of Pennsylvania Law School.

"Throughout his life, he was prominently identified with commercial, financial, cultural and philanthropic organizations of the community.The bulk of his estate was bequeathed to Wilkes College. He also left to the College all prints, books, paintings, and manuscripts regarding the history of Northeastern Pennsylvania."

Why Gilbert McClintock never married was puzzling. In addition to the town house subsequently bequeathed to Wilkes College, he owned a magnificent residence on the mountain top about ten miles east of Wilkes-Barre. His mountain home contained some beautiful paintings. One we particularly remember was a George Innes original of the Delaware Water Gap.

Gilbert was a client of mine for some years. At one point, he asked me to work with the Trust Department of his bank in the same manner that I worked with the competing bank. I told him I would be flattered, but was denied this privilege because the competing bank would not permit my dual role. Gilbert was furious and wanted to visit the other institution to "tell them off," but I persuaded him not to.

One of Gilbert's many wonderful accomplishments in later years was the publication of a beautiful book, *Valley Views of Northeastern Pennsylvania.* I am the proud owner of a volume inscribed by the author. The title page reads as follows:

VALLEY VIEWS
OF NORTHEASTERN PENNSYLVANIA

Reproductions of early prints and paintings of the Wyoming and other valleys of the Susquehanna, Lehigh, Delaware and Lackawana rivers together with a descriptive list of the plates: By Gilbert S. McClintock.

This lovely book, with its reproductions of rare and beautiful paintings, shows something of Gilbert McClintock's love of and devotion to the area. It was a rare privilege and honor to have known him, and to have shared his confidence. "He is great who is what he is from nature and who never reminds us of others," Emerson wrote in his "Essay on Great Men." Gilbert McClintock was such a man.

DR. EUGENE S. FARLEY

1899 –

I have come to know intimately so many outstanding men in Wilkes-Barre that it is difficult to place them in proper perspective and impossible to rate them. But I would have to include Dr. Eugene Shedden Farley, affectionately known as "Gene." Founder and President of Wilkes College, he has performed miracles in the field of education. Starting with nothing but a dream – no money, no facilities, no backlog to speak of – he has built a splendid college with a present enrollment of about 3600 students.

Originally, the school was called Bucknell Junior College. Within eleven years, by dint of Herculean effort and bulldog tenacity, it was in a position to qualify as an accredited college. This was in 1947. Dr. Farley persuaded Wilkes-Barre residents to bequeath to the college their fine old residences facing the Susquehanna River. They became classrooms, dormitories, and laboratories. In the meantime, this miracle man raised several million dollars, and today Wilkes College can boast of a new, modern gymnasium, an even more beautiful Fine Arts Building, and a library that would be the envy of any university in the nation. This impressive structure, costing nearly $2,000,000, was recently dedicated and inscribed:

THE
EUGENE SHEDDEN FARLEY
LIBRARY

May all who study in these halls gain vision to inspire, conviction to sustain, and wisdom to guide

Charles Waller, then chairman of the Board of Trustees, made this comment upon dedication:

"The Library is the heart of any college; it is, therefore, particularly appropriate that we dedicate this Library to Dr. Farley, who is in the very best sense the father of Wilkes College. The child of his heart and brain will ever gratefully acknowledge the parentage."

And from Fred M. Heckinger, Education Editor, *The New York Times,* November 1, 1968:

"Your college, after all, is the perfect example of a mission of service earnestly accepted and brilliantly carried off, not as a burden, but as an opportunity.

"... The years of seeing Gene Farley at work have persuaded me that he is a man of sound priorities ... The test is one of educational leadership and purpose – to add service to the other functions, but not indiscriminately, to what can be done well and honestly and without distortion ...

"... Eugene Farley is a man of priorities who has done much for this institution. He has not only shaped those within it, but he has shaped the community and the region around it as well. It speaks for itself. I need say no more about it. This is the purpose of higher education."

I could go on indefinitely singing the praises of this man and his achievements, but the eulogies of other acquaintances and friends must suffice.

Gene's lovely wife, Eleanor, also a brilliant scholar, died unexpectedly about two years ago. They were a devoted and companionable couple, and her death was a sudden and great loss for Gene. James Russell Lowell, wishing to pay tribute to a man he greatly admired, remarked, "The soil out of which such men as he are made is good to be born on, good to live on, good to die for and to be buried in." I know of no one for whom this description is more fitting than Eugene Shedden Farley.

There are so many outstanding citizens in Wilkes-Barre, but I must omit some. However, I should mention George T. Bell, who has done such a miraculous job with the Hospital Service Association of Northeastern Pennsylvania (Blue Cross). He has accomplished miracles and has been called to Jordan, Jamaica, and Puerto Rico to establish Blue Cross in those countries.

CHAPTER FOUR

POLICY FOR THE FIFTIES

By late 1949, my business had grown to quite a sizable one, with many clients scattered over a dozen states and a few abroad. It included some banks, churches, colleges, and an insurance company as well as individuals. It was my feeling that these clients should be kept up to date on my thinking – what prompted the investment policy I was advising. I therefore sent out policy letters from time to time. The ones reprinted here give an indication of what was happening in the stock and bond markets, and in the economy as a whole, during the years from 1950 to 1960.

October 21, 1949:

"Devaluation of the pound sterling, announced on September 18th, climaxed a summer of growing acuteness of the British situation. There was no alternative left save devaluation. Though a move of such magnitude coming so suddenly is unprecedented, American security and commodity markets took the news with relative calm. Twenty-five additional foreign countries quickly followed England and devalued their currencies in relation to the dollar.

"By itself, however, devaluation may accomplish very little. To capitalize on its full possibilities will require a high level of courage on the part of all concerned. Strong pressure against England's program has already materialized. Some of this may be politically difficult to resist, such as union pressures for increased wages and benefits. Some companies abroad will be tempted to increase export prices toward the original dollar level instead of expanding output in line with their new opportunities. Others may consider it more advantageous to divert exports to their domestic markets for price reasons. Only a resolute effort to enlarge production, control costs, and hold down prices in foreign markets can mobilize sufficient competitive weight to increase dollar exports above pre-devaluation levels.

"BOND MARKET:

"There is no indication of any real change in interest rates for the long term. The outlook, I believe, is for stability to mild strength in high-grade bonds. However, between now and December the government will have to prepare a program for a large refunding operation. Therefore, it might be advisable to defer for a while the purchase of long governments. It is conceivable that this refunding operation could bring about a slight reaction in long bonds.

"STOCK MARKET:

"One factor that has lately brought more investors into the stock market is the inflationary atmosphere created in the past six months, with a return to deficit financing and the increased spending by the government generally. Investors feel that this will further dilute purchasing power and lead to devaluation of the American dollar. Devaluation is certainly not in the cards for the near term, although it may come eventually. Nevertheless, this fear of inflation can conceivably send stock prices higher. For the past six months our government has been making efforts, by such means as wage policies and easing credit, to establish a sound structure. Through these artificial stimulants, Washington may succeed in sustaining it for some time. So we may have an extension of the present business boom which could last for another year or two. This would happen by more and more plant programs being completed, more and more new high-priced cars being supplied to buyers, and more and more houses being finished at still higher costs. It remains to be seen how long the government continues to encourage such a process."

September 27, 1950:

"Stocks have had a substantial rally during the past sixty days. The market as a whole is as high as it was before the outbreak of hostilities in Korea, and some groups, such as oils and rails, are considerably higher. There are three major reasons for this strength:

1) We are obviously faced with more inflation.
2) Good equities yield twice as much as bonds.
3) Most companies are reporting record earnings.

"Whether or not World War III is just around the corner is anybody's guess; it seems inevitable sooner or later. In the meantime, our government will continue to spend billions for defense, and we will have higher taxes. And we will have more inflation.

"The wartime fiscal record of the United States in the past hundred years may be summed up rather simply: WE DO NOT FIGHT DEFLATIONARY WARS. During the Civil War the National Banking System was legislated into existence, with a provision which facilitated the sale of United States Treasury securities to the banks. The government also resorted to the inflationary device of an inconvertible note issue.

"By 1915 deposits in the commercial banks had reached a total of $15 billion. As a result of World War I, deposits doubled in five years. In World War II they soared from $49 billion to $124 billion between 1940 and 1945. Government fiscal policies were largely responsible for these sensational increases in bank credit. This is the financial record of our wartime bull markets. There is as yet no evidence we are going to change this record.

"In the past, the stock market has had a severe decline with the actual outbreak of war, and then an advance to levels substantially higher than those prevailing at the outbreak of hostilities. Therefore, if we declared war against Russia tomorrow, I believe stock prices would go off substantially as they did following Pearl Harbor. Nevertheless, if you are not overextended in equities, I would suggest retention of all good common stocks.

"In view of the threat of additional inflation, I believe that investors should increase their holdings in good equities. However, where one has fifty percent or more of his funds in equities, I think any additional purchases should be deferred, since stock averages are high and the market is vulnerable to unfavorable news. Better buying opportunities may occur between now and the end of the year. Following November elections we are apt to get some distasteful controls and regulations and, of course, business is faced with an excess profits tax."

October 24, 1951:

"I believe the following major trends provide some background for long range investments:

1. *Inflation or Depreciation of the Dollar*

It has been substantial; will probably continue. Best defense for investor is the purchase of companies with assets in the ground or raw materials such as oils, metals, papers, natural gas.

2. *Rising Wages*

Substantial increases; will remain high and probably continue upward. Investors should seek stocks of companies with (a) low labor factor, such as oils, chemicals, drugs, metals; and (b) companies manufacturing labor-saving devices, such as office equipment, materials handling equipment.

3. *Corporate Taxes*

May be nearing a ceiling, but will continue high. Protection to be found in stocks where companies have (a) depletion allowances such as oils, metals and natural gas; and (b) where growth or expansion of dollar revenues is so great that growth in per share earnings will continue – such as drugs, chemicals, manufacturers of armament.

4. *New Industries*

New industries and products are constantly providing profit opportunities and rendering obsolete established businesses that have been profitable for years. For example, television vis à vis radio; titanium, already established in paint, and its prospects as a metal; fibreglass; synthetic yarns vis à vis cotton and wool; plastics; atomic power versus coal; the trucking industry as opposed to the railroads. There are many special investment situations arising in this category, but the industry which stands out is the chemicals. Many believe that this industry, despite its tremendous growth, is yet in its early youth, if not its infancy.

5. *Shifts in Consumer Income and Living Habits*

There has been a considerable publicity given the wide gains in income of the vast group earning between $2,000 and $5,000 annually. This increase has broadened the market for consumer durable goods, and particularly automobiles, which in turn broadens the demand for petroleum, automobile replacement parts and tires. Packaging is in a strong growth trend, stimulated by the supermarket. Likewise, and contributing to packaging growth, is the trend toward less time for preparation of meals through the use of frozen foods."

March 30, 1951:

"Fear of inflation has been a big factor in the strength of the stock market during the past year. For the long pull, in my opinion, it will continue to be an important factor, and it is something that the investor must not forget in formulating his long-term investment program.

"For the next few months we may be in for a little deflation, or at least a temporary halt to inflation. Nevertheless, I am of the opinion that for the long pull, there will be more inflation and that good equities will afford the greatest protection against it.

"Over the next few weeks, we may see an irregular stock market, with prices declining moderately. Earnings are still very high and will continue to be high during 1951 and 1952. Yields on good common stocks are still twice as much as yields on good bonds. Legislation to allow New York life insurance companies to purchase equities places another big cushion underneath the market.

"I believe it is still sound for the conservative investor to hold a big percentage of his capital in good, well-selected common stocks and to disregard intermediate swings in market prices."

June 24, 1952:

"The feature of the bond market last week was the new offering of U. S. Treasury 2-3/8's of 1958. Subscriptions were received greatly in excess of the amount offered and the new notes immediately sold at a premium.

"Corporate borrowing continues to be heavy, and consequently, recent new offerings have not been too successful. There is quite a backlog of unsold new issues, and since considerable financing is pending, I see no reason to expect any firming of the bond market.

"Stock prices reached a new high in the recovery movement last week, and by the close of the current week, were moderately higher. On balance, forces in support of higher common stock prices appear to be somewhat stronger, and we believe that the near-term market outlook continues to be relatively favorable. Careful selection is still essential, but good stocks do not appear to be high in relation to prospective earnings and dividends."

November 18, 1952:

"Eisenhower's election was a highly significant event. I doubt if the American public will appreciate its full significance until after his inauguration. For in this election, the American people decided against the trend toward socialism for a government that would act as the servant of all citizens.

"Business will be relieved from many burdensome restrictions. The excess profits tax is not likely to be renewed when it expires next June 30. We will have a sane and sound fiscal policy and a balanced budget. Dictatorship by the labor unions will diminish. Business will have more confidence; therefore, dividend policies will be more liberal.

"The election of Eisenhower will not solve all of our problems, because we must continue with our defense program, and government expenditures will remain high. But his election will give investors confidence such as they have not had for years.

"With this background I am compelled to remain optimistic on the market and am willing to keep a high percentage of money invested in good common stocks."

January, 1953:

"Stocks have had a substantial rise since the election, and while they may work somewhat higher, it is time for caution. I would not reach for stocks unless one sees something that is definitely undervalued. Where any of my clients have 80% or over in equities, I am going to start cutting back a little and nail down a few profits. However, the long-term outlook is good, and I would not advise any conservative investor to have less than 60% in common stocks. For comparative purposes, I have compiled some facts and figures dealing primarily with the year 1952.

1. In 1952, with 7% of the world's people, the U. S. produced 52% of the world's mechanized energy and made 65% of the world's manufactured goods.

2. In 1952, the U. S. achieved a Gross National Product of $350 billion, the greatest in its history.

3. During the year, our population increased 3 million – 50% more than estimated. By 1975, our population is apt to be 200 million. Prosperity by population has become one of the most important dynamics of United States growth.

4. In spite of certain controls, 1,100,000 new homes were completed – second biggest year on record.

5. Personal income after taxes soared to a record $235 billion, a gain of $9 billion over 1951.

6. Dividends paid out were $9.3 billion versus $9 billion in 1951.

7. The Dow-Jones Industrial Average reached 289.65, highest in twenty-two years, and was selling for only twelve times earnings versus twenty times in 1929.

8. In the seven post-war years, private industry has invested the staggering total of $151 billion on new plants. This is greater than all of the capital equipment of England, France and West Germany combined.

9. In 1952 we had forty-three million automobiles, one for every four people. In 1932 we had twenty-one million, one for every six.

10. In 1952 we had one telephone for every three people versus one for every seven in 1932. Incidentally, the world's largest privately owned enterprise, the $12 billion American Telephone & Telegraph

Company and its associated operating companies, added one new telephone every four seconds during each working day of 1952. As the new year started there were approximately forty million Bell telephones in service. People throughout the country are using them at the rate of 149 million conversations daily.

11. In 1952 90% of labor was covered by pension systems versus 15% in 1932. Pension plans now are estimated at 14,000, covering more than ten million workers. In 1930 we had about 700 pension plans.

12. An estimated $12 billion has already accumulated in private pension plans, and they are growing at the rate of $2 billion per year. Just try and guess what the size of all our pension plans will be in another twenty-five years."

July 17, 1953:

"Today, after two more years of high prosperity and record dividends, the Dow-Jones Industrial Average is in the neighborhood of 270. However, with many people predicting that the long-expected post-war recession will finally arrive next year, I find that some of my clients feel today much as they did in July, 1951.

"I am willing to concede that business may well be at a lower level next year than it is today, and I therefore intend to sell a few common stocks if the market should have a good rally later this year. However, I do not intend to go very far in this direction. Regardless of any recession or lack of recession in 1954, the rapid growth of this nation's technology and population (the latter is increasing at the rate of three cities the size of Boston annually) makes me a long-range "bull on America." I therefore hesitate to incur the penalties – capital gains taxes, brokerage fees, loss of income – involved in selling good common stocks.

"That the market is not overvalued at the present time is pretty well proven by the figures below:

	1929	1937	1946	1953
Cost of buying $1,000 worth of earnings	$19,110	$16,920	$15,590	$10,950
Cost of buying $1,000 worth of dividends	29,900	22,000	28,400	17,300
Cost of buying $1,000 worth of book value	(not avail.)	2,200	1,620	1,260

Cost of stocks that would give the same income as $1,000 worth of high grade bonds	1,560	1,075	900	675

October 22,1953:

"During the past month we have witnessed a remarkable recovery in prices for all types of bonds – government, corporate and tax-free. While we may have seen the highest prices to be expected in this recovery movement, it is quite obvious that officials in Washington are determined not to let prices slide again for quite some time. There are substantial amounts of government bonds maturing in 1954, and official Washington is anxious to lengthen the maturities of all new offerings as much as possible. Consequently, I believe that we can look for a stable bond market for several months to come.

"Prices for stocks have also risen considerably during the past two weeks. The rise has been selective, with electrical equipment, food, merchandising and other defensive stocks showing the most strength. Steel stocks also staged a good recovery. I expect the market to continue to be a fairly selective one, with prices generally apt to work a little higher this fall. Excellent yields are still obtainable in quality stocks, and dividends for 1953 will exceed those in 1952 by at least 5%.

"With the excess profits tax expiring December 31, earnings for many companies will be as good in 1954 as in 1953, even though we experience a 10% to 15% decline in business. I see no reason to disturb good quality stocks and in some cases I am willing to purchase stocks at present levels. Public utility stocks, natural gas stocks, and bank stocks are reasonably priced. Rubber stocks also look attractive for a good yield, and as a special situation Scott Paper has great attraction as a growth stock."

May 27, 1954:

"For the long pull, I think prices will remain fairly stable, and I believe money should be invested as it becomes available. The stock market continues to make new highs and at this point a technical reaction is certainly due. However, barring war in Indochina, it is my feeling that the market has not yet reached the peak. The new tax bill, if passed, will be very bullish. Earnings are holding up surprisingly well and so are dividends. In my opinion, the good high grade stocks are not overpriced.

"It has been obvious that stocks have been going into strong hands. To prove this I quote below from this week's issue of 'Barron's':

'Never in the history of the stock market has so big an advance in so short a period – 70 points by the Industrial Average in eight months – occurred with so little use of bank credit. At the end of last September, about a fortnight after the September 14 market bottom, customers' debit balances totaled $1,590 million. At the end of this April the amount owed was only $158 million higher, at $1,748 million. In the same seven months, however, customer credit balances jumped $145 million, or from $674 to $819 million. Thus, net borrowings on stocks between September 30, 1953, and April 30, 1954, rose a trifling $13 million, while the total value of listed stocks increased by over $24 billion (from $110.5 billion to $134.6 billion). In the light of the above, how anyone can construe the 1954 market performance as 'unhealthy' is hard to understand.'

"Recent figures released show that all corporations (exclusive of banks and insurance companies) have a working capital position of about $93 billion dollars at the end of 1953. This is up over $3 billion dollars in the past year and is an increase of about $27 billion dollars in the past five years. This vast sum of money provides plenty of capital for normal expansion and also means, in my opinion, more liberal dividends in 1954 than in 1953."

October 7, 1954:

"Yesterday the thirty Dow-Jones Industrial stocks ended the day at 364.43. This is the highest point reached since September, 1929, when this same Average stood at 369.97. It has risen over 100 points during the past year. Naturally, many investors are wondering if this market has gotten out of hand and if it is apt to have a big decline. For that reason I am writing you now to give you my views.

"Looking carefully at most stocks today, they do not appear overpriced in relation to present and future earnings and dividends. Of course, this market cannot be expected to continue on its upward path indefinitely. A good technical reaction is overdue, especially since some stocks look to be six months or so ahead of themselves, in anticipation of business, earnings, and dividend improvements. Unfavorable election news in November might create some temporary bearishness. Sudden flare-ups in Formosa or in other parts of the world could bring about some unsettlement. But a good reaction would be healthy and leave the market with a sounder footing.

"For the next two or three years, I see several things that could cause common stocks to move into higher ground. They are:

1) Defense expenditures of approximately $40 billion each year, necessitating deficit financing and lifting the National Debt to $300 billion. This will be very inflationary.

2) A continuation of an easy money policy by our government, which is inflationary.

3) A continuing trend of higher wages in all major industries, which is inflationary.

4) A tremendous expansion of our economy, in several fields, particularly atomic energy and electronics.

5) A great increase in our population, with a total of 175 million people estimated by 1960."

March 17, 1955:

"We live in the greatest nation in the world, and while our government is not perfect, it is functioning, on the whole, very satisfactorily. We have as our President a wonderfully public spirited citizen, with great ability. He is sound, he is conscientious, and if it is humanly possible to do so, he will keep us out of war. But he is keeping our defenses alert and ready. Our President, on the whole, has surrounded himself with a great Cabinet and with capable military leaders. The nation today is in a very strong position militarily and otherwise, and growing stronger each day. We are far ahead of Russia in the atomic and nuclear fields, and in the development of guided missiles – so much so that Russia is too smart to start a war. Our Senate and House, while not as perfect as we would like, will continue to back President Eisenhower on important legislation.

"We are faced with several years of great prosperity and with an era of peace. The President will continue to be friendly to business, and at the present time his popularity is at its highest peak. There is no one at the moment on the horizon who can defeat him in 1956.

"With this as a background, I feel that we will continue to have a strong market, and that investors who own good common stocks, bought at reasonable prices, should hold them."

April 20, 1956:

"During the past thirty days the stock market, as measured by the Dow-Jones Industrial Average, made an all-time high of 521. Many investors are wondering if present hight prices are justified, and what the market is apt to do from here.

"I have been consistently bullish on the market since May, 1949. I did not let the outbreak of the Korean War change my thinking. Nor did I let the end of the Korean crisis change my views. Again in September, 1953, when the market had a very sharp break, I maintained a bullish attitude and bought stocks on balance.

"During Eisenhower's illness I refused to do any selling and advised my clients to sit tight.

"We are, in my opinion, headed for a decade of unparalleled growth. The rapid growth of our population, the many and new dynamic industries that are springing up, and the vast amount of money being spent on new plant and equipment all point to an expanding and prosperous economy for several years, barring war.

"Inflation is rearing its ugly head again. One sees it on all sides, in price increases and wage increases. Furthermore, one cannot see anything to halt the trend. This strengthens our belief that, in the next few years, an equity in America's strong corporations will be preferable to cash.

"With the outlook for the next decade so encouraging, one must guard against loss of investment perspective. Checking the prices of one's stocks daily is a great American game, something like following the batting average of a favorite ball player. But the former game may be dangerous, leading the investor to overlook his long-range objectives, and to become emotional about his securities. Those who want to sell a stock (bought for long-range investment) just because it rose one or two points the day before, or who reprimand themselves for *not* having sold a stock which fell one or two points yesterday, generally achieve poor investment results. Nor do they achieve much peace of mind, because, when their stocks stand still. they worry most of all."

July 19, 1956:

"There is little that can be said about the bond market. Money remains fairly tight and bond prices fluctuate a little from day to day, depending to a certain extent on the number and amount of new issues being offered. There is no reason to expect any change in this pattern for the time being.

"Measured by the Dow-Jones Industrial Average, stocks are again approaching the high point of 521 reached last April. At this writing there are many reasons to believe that they will go through that level in the very near future. President Eisenhower's decision to run again has been a bullish factor; the threat of more inflation, another; and third is the growing recognition that industrial expansion, here and abroad, is going to continue for several years at an accelerated pace. To me this all means higher prices for good stocks as we go into 1957. . . .”

October 25, 1956:

“Reports from business are generally favorable. Earnings reports released thus far for the first nine months reveal higher earnings, but the year-to-year gain has narrowed progressively as compared with the results for the first half and the first quarter of 1956. On the whole, earnings in 1956 will be at least as good as 1955.

“But the stiffening of money rates will act as a real deterrent to any further market strength, except in special situations. While I have not changed my mind on the long-term outlook for the market, I do think that the investor should be cautious and deliberate today in the investment of new money. I would not disturb present holdings where sales would entail substantial capital gains . . . .”

December, 1956:

“A fair test of a successful investment is relative performance in both dividend growth and market price. In the Thirties investors who concentrated on “blue chips” stressed consumer goods stocks, bank stocks, and gold mining shares, groups which enjoyed the highest investment ratings in those days. Actually, they did quite well for a number of years in relation to such now popular groups as the oils, papers and steels – which at that time were considered speculative. However, the error in having stuck dogmatically to a policy of “buying the blue chips and forgetting them” is dramatically shown in the following table, which lists a number of the most highly regarded and widely held investments of twenty years or more ago. As a measure of relative market performance, we have shown both market price and the percentage of the Dow-Jones Industrial Average which that price represented in the periods covered.

“It is of further interest to note that growth in earnings for the Dow-Jones Industrials has outpaced the increase in both market price and dividends. While the latter are, on the average, up a little over three times, earnings have gone from $8.58 in the 1935-39 period to $35.57 estimated for 1955, a better than four-fold increase.

“The principal conclusion which we draw is that investing requires constant supervision and adaptation to the continuously changing conditions characteristic of our dynamic economy. Blue chips can also suffer from obsolescence, and to invest in them and forget them can be as dangerous a policy today as it has proven to have been in the past. In our opinion, the most successful investors have been those who have

Period 1935-1939				1956		
Mean Price	Average Dividend	Price as % of Dow-Jones		Current Price	Ind. Dividend	Price as % of Dow-Jones
34	$1.86	24.1	American Chicle	61	$ 3.00	12.6
27	1.15	19.2	American Can	48	2.00	10.0
151	9.00	106.3	American Tel & Tel	181	9.00	37.6
110	4.05	77.8	Coca Cola	125	5.00	26.0
21	1.00	14.7	Corn Products	28	1.30	5.7
37	2.06	25.9	General Foods	89	3.40	18.4
54	5.00	38.3	Homestake Mining	37	2.00	7.7
22	0.72	15.7	International Harvester	37	2.00	7.6
102	5.60	72.1	Liggett & Myers	69	5.00	14.3
27	1.72	19.1	National Biscuit	40	2.00	8.3
49	2.40	35.0	Woolworth	49	2.50	10.1
56	2.16	39.4	Guaranty Trust	81	3.70	16.7
32	1.00	22.4	First National City	63	2.60	13.0
44	2.98	31.4	Chesapeake & Ohio	55	3.50	11.4
142	6.29	100.0	Dow-Jones Ind. Average	482.72	19.50	100.00

kept their portfolios in tune with the times rather than those who because of inertia, sentimentality or excessive attention to tax considerations have been unwilling to shift their holdings as conditions change."

February 27, 1957:

"In late October, 1956, and again in January, 1957, we suggested that the Dow-Jones Industrial Average might recede to 450 sometime during the first quarter of 1957. Recently, it struck a low of 458, and is now at about 470. We may yet see the Average go to 450, or a little lower. However, to us, this isn't a decline sufficient to cause undue concern.

"Last year at this time there was bullishness on all sides. Today, if one listens enough and reads enough, he encounters considerable pessimism. In our opinion, this bearishness is being overdone and stems mainly from Wall Street boardrooms. Much of the selling has come from the small, uninformed investor who frightens easily. Quick to sense such a change in sentiment, the professional traders have taken advantage of the situation, and have aided and abetted the decline.

"In our opinion it is no time to get bearish. A certain amount of restraint and caution is in order; but don't lose your long-term perspective because we are having a normal healthy correction in our market."

June 28, 1957:

"Severe declines in prices of all fixed, interest-bearing securities have occurred during the past month. For the first time since 1929 we have seen public utility bonds offered with a 6% and a 6 1/4% coupon. Money seems to be tighter than ever. Federal Reserve officials seem determined not to change their present policy. It begins to look as if these high interest rates are here to stay, and it is possible that the bond market will go a little lower.

"Recently the market rallied to 510 in the Dow-Jones Industrial Average. During the past week, it has declined rather sharply to below 500. Undoubtedly the high yields afforded by bonds and preferred stocks have been a factor in the recent selloff. From now on these high interest rates may be quite a deterrent to higher stock prices. However, investors, large and small, are very conscious of inflation and the declining purchasing power of the dollar.

"We still urge clients to keep heavily invested in equities. The market remains highly selective, but we favor the following industries:

Electrical Equipment	Office Equipment
Papers	Chemicals
Oils	Public Utilities
Metals and Mining	Banks

November 29, 1957:

"Until President Eisenhower's illness was announced on Tuesday it appeared that the market was on the way to a good rally. His illness, as usual, brought about some hysterical selling late Tuesday. On Wednesday, the market regained all of Tuesday's loss. The action on Wednesday would indicate that we are in for a further rally. Assuming that we are not suddenly confronted with additional bad news, I would expect this rally to take the Dow-Jones Average up to around 450-460. (It is now at about 440.)

"If such a rally occurs I believe it would be sound to take a more defensive position, because I expect the Average sometime before Spring to be down again around the 400 level. Business may start to improve by then, but there is no assurance that earnings will improve. And it is *earnings power* that is the fundamental market force.

"Business, generally speaking, is a little worse than appears on the surface, and will decline further before any improvement is seen. It is not the time to get too bearish, but it is a time for caution.

"My advice, where clients are not too heavy in equities, is to sit tight with good sound common stocks, but not to be in a hurry to make new purchases. The long-term trend is still bullish and the inflationary spiral has not been permanently stopped. It has been halted temporarily."

October 28, 1958:

"There are several reasons why the current bull market may rise another 10% to 20%, yet basic long-range factors point to a very probable 'day of reckoning.' What is the investor to do now? There is, of course, no one answer for all portfolios. However, our advice to the average investor, with well-bought securities, is to keep 70% to 80% of his funds in common stocks, for inflation protection and in expectation that the bull market is not yet fully mature. We feel that the other 20% to 30% of the average portfolio should contain fixed income securities, both for the good yields obtainable and as protection against the possibility that one will not act soon enough if and when a major reversal in the stock market occurs.

"It is our opinion that public utility stocks provide the safest haven for new equity investments."

June 25, 1959:

"The factors which have led us to view the stock market constructively thus far in 1959 – booming business, belief that our nation is continuing to grow, and our price level continuing to inch upward – are still at work. Moreover, we continue to feel that many individual common stocks represent sound value at present prices. However, with the spread between average stock and bond yields now favoring the latter by 1.9% (3.1% vs. 5%), we feel that the market in general is adequately discounting the reasons for owning common stocks. Therefore, we think now is a good time to invest some 'backlog' funds in long-term bonds."

September 25, 1959:

"The bond market has had a substantial decline in the past month, simply because the demand for money exceeds the supply. The discount rate has been raised to 4% and the rate on 'prime' loans to 5%.

"There have been three main factors behind the weakness of the stock market since Labor Day. As stated in last month's letter, we feel that two of these factors – the steel strike and Khrushchev's visit – are not valid reasons for bearishness. The third item, the height of interest rates, must be taken more seriously. This worries common stockholders for two reasons: (1) good bonds currently yield about two percent more than good stocks, and (2) a money market panic could end the current boom.

"It is our feeling that the yield discrepancy between bonds and stocks, while almost unprecedented, is justified by the excellent state of business and by the nation's anticipated rate of growth, both real and inflationary. We do not feel that high interest rates are likely to cause a recession. They are slowing the rate of home building somewhat, and deferring certain municipal projects. But we doubt if other segments of the economy will be seriously affected, since money, while expensive, is still available.

"In view of the above, we feel that most of the market correction may have already occurred. A good many individual equities have fallen near what we consider buying levels."

As we concluded the 1950 – 1960 decade, we naturally wondered about the decade to come, and what it would hold in store. President Eisenhower could not seek a third term; he had been extremely popular, and his popularity could prove to be very helpful to the

Republican nominee. Vice-President Nixon at the moment seemed to have the inside track as the Republican candidate, but on the Democratic side there were several possibilities – John F. Kennedy, Lyndon B. Johnson, and possibly Hubert H. Humphrey.

The Dow-Jones Industrial Average closed the year 1959 at 679. At the beginning of 1950, it had stood at 200. Could it do that well in the next decade?

PART FIVE

1960-1970

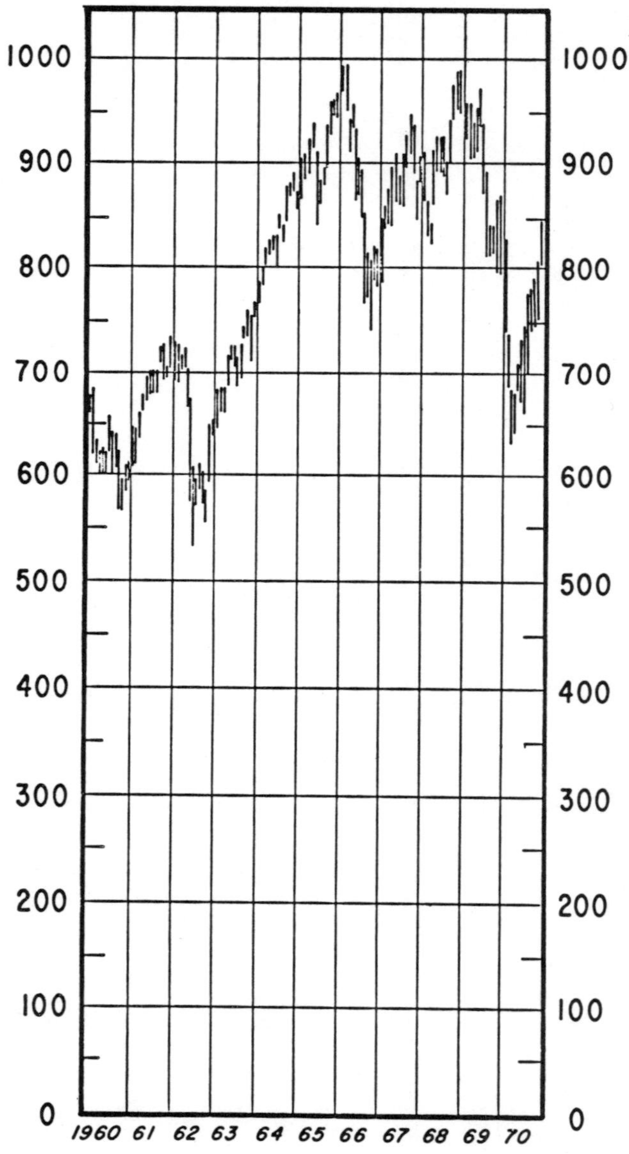
1000
900
800
700
600
500
400
300
200
100
0
1960 61 62 63 64 65 66 67 68 69 70

CHAPTER ONE

JOHN FITZGERALD KENNEDY

President Eisenhower had brought some calm and tranquility to the nation, and for the most part, during the Fifties we experienced an era of peace. This atmosphere had created a strong stock market, and investors sought out equities with confidence. The 1960's, however, brought a decade of upheaval, tumult and violence.

In November of 1960, John Fitzgerald Kennedy was elected our thirty-fifth President. At forty-three, he was our youngest elected President, and first Roman Catholic to hold this office, defeating Richard Milhous Nixon by the narrow margin of 100,000 votes.

In his inaugural address, President Kennedy said, "The torch has been passed to a new generation. Let this word go forth from this time and place to friend and foe alike that the torch has been passed to a new generation of Americans – born in this century, tempered by war, disciplined by a hard and bitter peace, proud of our ancient heritage." To American citizens, he said, "Ask not what your country can do for you, but what you can do for your country;" to the world, "Ask not what America will do for you, but what together we can do for the freedom of man."

He at once inaugurated a program labeled "The New Frontier," which called for federal aid to education, medicare for the aged under social security, enlargement of civil rights through executive action, aid to depressed areas, and accelerated space exploration. He established the Peace Corps, with its hundreds of young volunteers undertaking goodwill missions in foreign countries. With his youth and enthusiasm, President Kennedy seemed to convince Americans that we were going to move forward with confidence and assurance.

But certain statements he made indicated that he was aware, as well, of the serious problems that faced our nation and the world. One of his most significant – and prophetic – comments came in the first major address he made to Congress, on January 30, 1961: "We shall have to test anew whether a nation organized and governed such as ours can endure. The outcome is by no means certain. The answers are by no means clear." These words were not uttered lightly, and on an occasion prior to his assassination, he repeated them to the Congress.

Until his campaign for the Vice-Presidency in 1956, Kennedy had never been west of the Alleghenies. Born and reared in Boston, educated at Harvard and then resident of Great Britain for several years, he was distinctly an Easterner. Hence he did not know our nation in the way Truman and Eisenhower had known it.

He found the Presidency to be a greater and more complex responsibility than he had anticipated. There were times when the magnitude of his problems seemed almost to overwhelm him. But apparently he did recognize the explosive unrest that prevailed with minority groups and the problems inherent in poverty, as typified by our slums and ghettoes. He knew that unless we solved many of these problems in this decade, our nation as we had known it might not be able to survive.

We may never know whether the mood of change prevalent in the country was inaugurated by this young, idealistic President or whether he was simply swimming with the excitement that was already upon us.

One of his first mistakes, and one that caused him great anguish, occurred in April, 1961 – the humiliating failure of the invasion of Cuba which came to be known as "The Bay of Pigs Invasion." Kennedy leaned heavily on the advice given him by the C.I.A. and his military advisers in handling this unfortunate misadventure. Nonetheless, he shouldered the blame for what was a smashing defeat for both the President and the nation.

Anxious to establish better relations with the Soviet Union, Kennedy had arranged for a meeting in Vienna with Premier Khruschev in May, 1961. The outspoken Premier capitalized on the Bay of Pigs fiasco. The meeting was strained and unsuccessful.

How much this meeting influenced President Kennedy we may never know, but soon afterward he dispatched about 20,000 military advisers to South Vietnam. He subsequently made two public statements regarding the situation there that are worth recording: "The training missions that we have in South Vietnam have been instructed that if they are fired upon they are, of course, to fire back to protect themselves." This was in February, 1962. In December, he observed: "We don't see the end of the tunnel. But I don't think it is darker than it was a year ago and in some ways it is lighter."

To illustrate how little we knew of the dangers that lay ahead, General Paul D. Harkins remarked soon afterward, "The South Vietnam armed forces have now attained the experience, training and necessary equipment required for victory."

When President Kennedy took office in 1961, we were in the midst of a business recession. Unemployment was up to 7%, higher than at any time during Eisenhower's last four years. Our balance of payments deficit in 1960 had reached a figure of nearly $4,000,000,000, and our outflow of gold to other countries was approaching $2,000,000,000.

What of the market? In the fall of 1961 the Dow-Jones Industrial Average had reached a high of 734.91. By June 1962 it was as low as 535.76, a decline of 28%. Some of this slump could be attributed to the business recession underway and some of it to a disillusionment on the part of many businessmen concerning some of Kennedy's policies. This was best illustrated in April of 1962, when the steel industry, without consulting the White House, announced a price increase. Kennedy was infuriated and issued the following statement: "In this serious hour in our nation's history, when we are confronted with grave crises in Berlin and Southeast Asia, when we are devoting our energies to economic recovery and stability . . . at a time when restraint and sacrifice are being asked of every citizen, the American people will find it hard, as I do, to accept a situation in which a tiny handful of steel executives, whose pursuit of private power and profit exceeds their sense of public responsibility, can show such utter contempt for the interest of 185 million Americans."

Not satisfied with the castigation, he unfortunately went further by commenting to aides, "My father always told me that steel men were sons of bitches." Steel men were understandably furious, and a reply was delivered by Allison R. Maxwell, Jr., President of the Pittsburgh Steel Company, before the American Iron and Steel Institute: "In this serious hour in our nation's history, when we are confronted with grave crises abroad, when our government is asking servicemen to risk their lives, I am sure you will find it hard, as I do, to accept a situation in which a tiny handful of government officials, in their pursuit of monopoly power over business and industry, undermine the profit system that has made our nation great, and the very Constitutional freedoms they have sworn to uphold."

In September, 1962, the discovery was made that the Russians had established missile sites in Cuba. Naturally this caused great concern, and was one of the contributing factors in the market's sharp decline. In October our government took decisive action. Naval vessels were dispatched to Cuban waters and a complete blockade of the island was effected. In the meantime, Russia was ordered to remove all missile sites by a given date or see Cuba invaded by the United States.

President Kennedy had the great satisfaction of dictating these terms to Khrushchev and of having the U. S. S. R. accede to our demands.

During late 1962 the nation was greatly heartened by our successful stand over Cuba. The market lifted accordingly, in what is known as a "confidence rally." Shortly before Christmas, Castro released over a thousand prisoners who had been captured and held for ransom during 1961's ill-fated "Bay of Pigs Invasion." By early 1963, all offensive weapons had apparently been removed from Cuba and the missile sites destroyed.

One of Kennedy's recommendations in his initial appearance before Congress was to step up the national space program. For the first time in history, three orbital passes were made around the planet by Captain John Glenn on February 20, 1962. America's space effort paid a further dividend later in the year when the communications satellite "Telstar" went into orbit. These two events were profoundly significant. Future generations may well regard the year 1962 as the most revolutionary year of the twentieth century.

As we went into 1963, President Kennedy pressed for a civil rights bill, a reformed tax program and other important legislative measures – most of them badly needed. His rapport with Congress was not great nor their relationship overly cordial, and very few of his programs were enacted prior to his assassination. "His gifts of cultivated speech, his graceful form and elegance, aroused their admiration and sometimes even their envy, but he was never a leader of the Congress in the Johnsonian sense."[1]

Paradoxically, following John Kennedy's assassination, President Johnson was able, in a few short weeks, to get action from Congress on almost the entire Kennedy program. "The whole psychology of the Capital City therefore has been changed by the cruel events of the past week. The program is the same. President Johnson did not alter a single line in it today, but the mind and spirit of the city have been transformed. This is the terrible paradox and tragedy of the moment, for President Kennedy apparently had to die to create a sympathetic atmosphere for his program."[2]

John Fitzgerald Kennedy was murdered in Dallas, Texas, on November 22, 1963. Nothing comparable to it, in this century, had brought the nation to such a state of abject sadness and shock. How

1. James Reston, *Sketches in the Sand.* New York: Alfred A. Knopf, 1967, pp. 382-383. Used by permission.

2. *Ibid,* p. 383

could such a horrible deed be enacted in a country such as ours? Little did we realize that it would be followed in the years to come by similar killings, and by riots and destruction of property.

CHAPTER TWO

LYNDON BAINES JOHNSON

On November 22, 1963, the new President took the oath of office in the cabin of the airliner that was to carry home the body of the murdered President, and both families, on the return journey to Washington. After the swearing-in ceremony, the new President had this message for the nation: "This is a sad time for all people. We have suffered a loss that cannot be weighed. For me it is a deep personal tragedy. I know the world shares the sorrow that Mrs. Kennedy and her family bear. I will do my best. This is all I can do. I ask for your help – and God's."

No one can deny that Lyndon Baines Johnson stepped into the office of the Presidency in extremely difficult and troubled times. Johnson was born and reared in the hill country of western Texas, of parents who were anything but affluent. He was dynamic and ambitious – very ambitious politically. Graduating from Southwestern Texas University, he was elected to the House of Representatives in 1936. Later elected to the U. S. Senate, he became Democratic Senate Majority Leader and under the wise guidance of Samuel Rayburn was subsequently to become the most powerful man in the Senate. Not always loved by members of the Senate, he was highly respected and admired – admired for his ability to get important legislation through by arm twisting and tough language. "President Kennedy's eloquence was designed to make men think; President Johnson's hammer blows are designed to make men act."[3]

"Lyndon Baines Johnson is to the politics of America what the State of Texas is to the other states. He is a gargantuan figure: he is a whopper. Measuring him for history is like measuring an active volcano with an inch tape. He barbecues people who try, and eats them for breakfast."[4]

"Kennedy came to the White House wondering out loud whether a country governed such as ours could endure. Johnson could no more

---

3. *Ibid,* p. 386
4. *Ibid,* p. 390

think or say that than he could denounce Lady Bird or the flag."[5]

We must remember that Johnson lost his campaign for his party's Presidential nomination in 1960 largely because of the national prejudice against Southerners. He was embittered by this, but was finally persuaded by Kennedy to accept the Vice-Presidential nomination for the sake of party unity.

President Kennedy, as we know, was an Eastern intellectual – Johnson a plainspoken Southerner with a distinct dislike for intellectuals. This did not make for a harmonious situation, even later, after Kennedy's death, when there were many Kennedy men who stayed in the administration. Johnson's long experience in the Senate stood him in good stead during his first months of office. Congressional leaders respected him and with little delay he was able to get many constructive measures made into laws. His energetic and skillful handling of Congress generally won him the support of the nation, including that of labor, business and agricultural leaders. This spirit was best exemplified by a remark made in June, 1965 by Jack Valenti, one of President Johnson's top aides: "I sleep each night a little better, a little more confidently, because Lyndon Johnson is my President." The shock and trauma so widespread following Kennedy's assassination had been largely dispelled.

Johnson approached the 1964 election with extreme confidence. There was never any real doubt that he would be the Democratic candidate. When the Republicans, torn by dissensions, nominated Barry Goldwater, this only served to reassure him further. He was anxious to win by the greatest majority of any Presidential aspirant, and he came close to it. His election victory was overwhelming, and with Hubert Humphrey as his hand-picked Vice-President, he was inaugurated January 20, 1965, in what appeared to be an optimistic and stable atmosphere.

But there was a dark cloud overhanging the scene that would eventually turn his great popularity into outspoken, bitter criticism. His standing with the citizenry ultimately sank to a level so low that in 1968, recognizing the trend, he withdrew as a candidate for reelection.

5. *Ibid,* p. 392

CHAPTER THREE

VIETNAM

In this writer's opinion, and in that of millions of our citizens, our entrance into Vietnam was one of the most profound mistakes this nation has ever made. It has been, as events came to prove, the longest and most expensive war in our history, placing a severe drain on our troubled financial picture. Additionally, it made us extremely unpopular throughout the world and divided our nation with a bitterness as deep-seated as that of the Civil War. President Johnson, as our leader, had ultimately to take almost all of the blame. In retrospect, it should be pointed out that it was President Kennedy who dispatched 20,000 advisers to Vietnam in 1961.

John Kenneth Galbraith, Ambassador to India under President Kennedy, wrote to the President on October 9, 1961: "Although at times I have been rather troubled by Berlin, I have always had the feeling that it would be worked out. I have continued to worry far, far more about South Vietnam. This is more complex, far less controllable, far more varied in the factors involved, far more susceptible to misunderstanding. And to make matters worse, I have no real confidence in the sophistication and political judgment of our people there. Harriman, incidentally, shares my view."[6]

On April 4, 1962, he wrote: "Keep up the threshold against the commitment of American combat forces. This is of the utmost importance – a few will mean more and more and more. And then the South Vietnamese boys will go back to the farms. We will do the fighting[7]..... We have a growing military commitment. This could expand step by step into a major, long, drawn-out, indecisive military involvement. We are backing a weak and, on the record, ineffectual government and a leader who as a politician may be beyond the point of no return[8]..... We should resist all steps which commit American

6. John Kenneth Galbraith, *Ambassador's Journal*. Boston: Houghton, Mifflin Co., p. 225. Used by permission.

7. *Ibid*, p. 344

8. *Ibid*, p. 342

troops to combat action and impress upon all concerned the importance of keeping American forces out of actual combat commitment."[9]

During his 1964 campaign, Lyndon Johnson remarked regarding Vietnam, "We are not about to send American boys 10,000 miles away from home to do what boys in Asia should do for themselves." A joint statement by General Maxwell Taylor and Defense Secretary Robert McNamara had been made in the fall of 1963: "The major part of the task of the United States can be completed by the end of 1965." In October, 1965, Hubert Humphrey commented: "The tide has turned, the Vietcong cannot win. They have been stopped." General William Westmoreland, speaking in November, 1967, observed that "We have reached an important point when the end begins to come into view." In a hearing before the Senate Foreign Relations Committee nearly fifteen years earlier, General Douglas MacArthur had remarked, "Only a lunatic would wish to use American ground forces in China."

Why were our leaders so mistaken in their judgments and why so misinformed in the facts needed to analyse this situation? Perhaps one of the gravest reasons was that of misjudging the amounts of aid that Vietnam would receive from Communist China and the U. S. S. R.

Soon after President Johnson's inauguration, the Vietcong stepped up its activities to the point where we had to either withdraw or escalate. Johnson decided on the latter, after receiving advice from members of his cabinet – particularly Defense Secretary Robert McNamara and Secretary of State Dean Rusk – that this was the course to pursue. General Westmoreland and his military advisers also concurred.

Whereas he opposed bombing North Vietnam while running for the Presidency, Johnson ordered the bombing shortly after his inauguration. To assure the American people of support backing this decision, he had several prominent members of his cabinet – McGeorge Bundy, Dean Rusk, and Robert McNamara – appear on television to second his actions.

More and more fighting men were sent to South Vietnam and hostilities were escalated at a rapid pace. Late in the summer of 1965, we were suddenly confronted with the news that the Vietcong had fired on two of our vessels in the Gulf of Tonkin. The President lost no time in approaching Congress and seeking permission to take any action necessary, not only in South Vietnam but in all Southeast Asia, to

9. *Ibid,* p. 342

oppose Communist aggression. Congress apparently felt it had little choice but to grant his request. There were only two dissenting votes – Senators Morse from Oregon and Gruening of Alaska. This was all that was necessary to escalate the war even more rapidly. Before the American public fully realized it, we had over 500,000 fighting men in South Vietnam, with casualties growing daily. We were now spending billions of dollars to prosecute the war effort; more and more, public opposition to it increased, and the nation's divisiveness on the subject grew deeper. As one authority said, a long and bitter ordeal amid war in a small southeastern nation spilled our blood and split the nation.

These events had a direct bearing on our stock market and complicated the duties of the Investment Counselor. One need only study the ups and downs of the Dow-Jones Industrial Average from 1965 through 1969 to see how widely stocks fluctuated. One really had to make decisions from day to day and from week to week. Naturally, our Gross National Product remained high, employment was the highest ever, spendable income had never been greater and inflation was rising sharply. All of these things had to be considered in making investment judgments. Most of my clients had tremendous profits in many securities, so always there were the capital gains taxes to consider when contemplating sales. Some industries were naturally doing better than others, so selectivity, as well as diversification, was important. I did not attempt to outguess the market too finely during 1965 and 1966, but I did do some selective selling in 1967. By and large, however, no major changes were made until June, 1969. At this time bond yields – corporate and tax exempt – were higher than at any time since the Civil War, and I switched some common stock money into bonds. An ensuing chapter will cover the developments in money rates and how they affected our markets.

How much the Vietnam situation contributed to a national spirit of violence culminating in riots such as those in Watts, and other cities, we shall never know. There were also the assassinations of Martin Luther King and Robert Fitzgerald Kennedy. No doubt it was a contributing factor. We do know that it caused many hundreds of youthful conscientious objectors to flee to Canada and Sweden, led to the public burning of draft cards, and on several occasions of our flag.

CHAPTER FOUR

DISSENSION, UNREST, REBELLION

The unrest in our large cities, leading to riots and looting, arose from long-suppressed resentments. Disenchantments by our large Negro populations in the ghettoes had long been smoldering. It was evident to close observers that generations of discrimination against the Negro would make the more militant leaders incite others to rebellion.

Probably the first and best remembered outbreak was the march on Selma, Alabama, led by Martin Luther King. This was closely followed by the murder of three white sympathizers in Mississippi. Then, out of the blue in the summer of 1966, we were made acutely aware of the turmoil underlying our domestic scene by the riots that occurred in Watts, the Negro area of Los Angeles. Few people dreamed that a city in this nation could so suddenly and decisively erupt into chaos. Before it was over thirty people had died, 900 were injured, and damage to property was estimated to run into the millions. It was several weeks before the authorities felt that the situation was under control.

One authority has said that Watts was probably the most important event of the 1960-1970 decade, overshadowing the assassination of President Kennedy. It told us in no uncertain terms that we had a potential revolution on our hands, with the Watts incident only a forerunner of the violence that would spring up around the nation; and events of 1967 and 1968 bore out the forebodings begun to be felt with this initial burst of violence. Cities like Washington, Chicago, Detroit and Newark would feel it next, and with far-reaching implications.

Following these outbreaks came the assassinations of Martin Luther King and of Robert Kennedy. These tragedies helped to spark student revolt in some of our larger universities, such as the University of California at Berkeley, Columbia, Harvard, Cornell, and many others. Some of it was racist, some rebellion against the "Establishment," and no doubt much of it opposition to the war in Vietnam.

In January, 1963, Governor of Alabama George Wallace commented in his inaugural address, "I draw the line in the dust and toss the gauntlet before the feet of tyranny, and I say, segregation now, segregation tomorrow, segregation forever." Speaking before the NAACP Convention in July of that year, Chicago Mayor Richard Daley made one of the more inept statements of the decade: "There are no ghettoes in Chicago." Needless to say, feeling ran high on both sides during the Sixties.

The 1960 – 1970 decade brought more unrest and dissension than any previous period in our history, including the Civil War. Sometimes it takes violence and revolution to correct the ills and miscarriages of justice. We may in later years feel that the events of the Sixties were necessary to bring about needed reforms.

CHAPTER FIVE

THE LABYRINTH COMPOUNDED BY EMOTIONS

The stock market's fairly drastic decline in 1962 was in reaction to the slight business recession as well as the Cuban crisis. It bounced back pretty quickly, and by the beginning of 1963 had regained nearly all of its loss. With the exception of some small corrections, it started on a merry climb, reaching an all-time high of 995.15 on February 9, 1966. In fact, during this day's session, it reached a figure of 1001.11.

During the 1950 – 1960 decade, corporate profits had risen gradually, with sufficient dips to keep businessmen and consumers cautious. During the 1960's, however, everything seemed to be going up, and investors and businessmen threw caution to the winds. The combined pressures of consumer spending, business expansion and the Vietnam War sent prices, wages and interest rates soaring, catching the nation up in an inflationary spiral that spread like a prairie fire.

Mass Psychology of Investors

When attempting to chronicle the great cyclical swings in our stock market, one should remember that the psychology of investors constitutes perhaps fifty percent of the factors at work. Economic and monetary factors are important, but it is *stock market sentiment* that drives stock markets to extremes – both up and down. I coined a phrase of my own to express this phenomenon: "When dealing with the stock market, you are talking about a labyrinth compounded by the emotions of millions of human beings."

In speaking of stock market gyrations, Charles MacKay, in his book, *Extraordinary Popular Delusions and the Madness of Crowds,* talked about "those little summer flies that all buzz around one spot, then shift to another and then go back again for no apparent reason – they just decide to move. I suspect human beings are like that, too." Once a speculative orgy starts, it feeds on itself, sooner or later reaching its peak and eventually falling on its face.

In *My Own Story,* Bernard Baruch observed, "What makes the task of fact finding so difficult is that in the stock market the facts of any situation come to us through a curtain of human emotions. What drives the prices of stocks up or down is not impersonal economic forces or changing events but the human reactions to these happenings. The constant problem of the investor or analyst is how to disentangle the cold, hard economic facts from the rather warm feelings of the people dealing with these facts."[10]

The advance from the early Fifties to 1966 was fueled by an environment characterized as one of growth and/or inflation. The current environment is the first one in two decades when a deflationary period prevailed. The greatest difference between the present decline and others of the past two decades is that fiscal and monetary actions are being taken in an attempt to correct the excesses of the past decade.

In December, 1968, the market reached a high of 985.21, after a low point of 825.13 earlier in the year. By the summer of 1969, it had rebounded to 968.85, then sold down to 769.93 by year-end. From these figures, it is easy to see that during 1966, 1967, 1968, and 1969, we experienced very erratic market moves. It was a difficult time for Investment Counselors. Consider these losses during 1969 and early 1970 by some major blue chips: duPont 92 ½, from 165 at the start of 1969; Atlantic Richfield from 135 to 44 7/8; U. S. Steel 30 3/8, down from 42; General Electric 50 ¼ versus 93; Standard Oil of New Jersey 49 7/8 from 78; and General Motors 59 ½, down from 79. American Telephone and Telegraph, the country's most widely-held stock, dropped slowly but steadily from 58 1/8 to 40 3/8.

Conglomerates had even greater declines. Some examples: Occidental Petroleum fell to 13 1/8 from 47; Litton to 16 1/8 from 72; Gulf and Western to 9½, down from 49; and LTV toppled to 7 1/8 from 95. To cite a perfect example of poor judgment and excessive speculation, LTV bought control of Jones and Laughlin Steel at 75. J & L later dropped to 11. LTV owns about 80% of the stock.

On the other hand, some of the glamor blue clips had large gains during this period. Such stocks as IBM, Burroughs, National Cash Register, Control Data, Polaroid, Johnson & Johnson, American Hospital Supply, Baxter Laboratories, Bard, Becton Dickenson, and many others had their own bull market. Therefore, it is easy to see that if one purchased the well-known blue chips and was unfortunate enough to get into the speculative conglomerates, he would have fared

10. Bernard Baruch, *My Own Story*. New York: Holt, Rinehart & Winston, 1957. Used by permission.

poorly. But if he had avoided these in favor of the high-multiple blue chip glamors, he could have done very well. I was fortunate enough to sell most of my clients' Litton between 110 and 80 and some duPont at the top, buying considerable amounts of Burroughs, IBM, and Baxter Laboratories. But because of large capital gains, I did little selling in the well-known blue chips or in the oil stocks that had a very large decline during the last part of 1969 and in early 1970.

What factors were at work during the last five years of the Sixties to make for such erratic markets? In the first place, we must realize that there was an excessive amount of rampant speculation. Investors became enamoured with the word "inflation" and felt that any common stock, without too much regard for price or earnings, would give him protection against inflation.

> No end of grief has been caused by the prevalent misconception that inflation pushes stock prices up. What pushes stock prices up is profits – and inflation, which means rising costs, is bad for profits. (Stocks and well-managed mutual funds are indeed a hedge against gradual inflation – but only from a strictly long-term standpoint. The assets and productive resources represented by a share of stock are "real" wealth, whose value increases over the years as the purchasing power of money declines.)[11]

The new issue market went wild in 1968 and part of 1969. Common stocks of young companies offered at $5 and $10 soared to 60 or 100, where they would be selling at 100 times earnings or more.

The stock of Kentucky Fried Chicken was offered at $15 in 1966. Earnings moved up from zero to $1.25 a share by 1969, adjusted for three stock splits. An investor purchasing 1,000 shares at the initial offering price would have seen his investment grow to 7,500 shares worth over $400,000 by 1969, when the stock reached 55.

In the early months of 1970, because of the general market decline as well as criticism by reputable accounting firms leveled at bookkeeping methods found in the franchising industry, the stock fell to 13½ – where the original investment would be worth $101,250. But in spite of the company's overexpansion and other problems, Kentucky Fried Chicken – with Colonel Harland Sanders as its popular trademark

11. *The New York Times Magazine*. August 31, 1969

is basically a sound operation with a popular product, and will probably recover and continue to do well as a division of Hueblein, Inc.

Backers of a firm in Nashville, Tennessee, Minnie Pearl's Chicken Systems, Inc., watched the spectacular success of Kentucky Fried Chicken and decided that such a franchise operation in the State of Tennessee could do equally well. Together with his brother and a group of wealthy Nashvilleans, John J. Hooker – narrowly defeated for Governor of Tennessee in 1966 – launched the company in 1967. They allowed friends and acquaintances to purchase stock at fifty cents a share. Minnie Pearl, the popular comedienne from Nashville, agreed to lend her name as a trademark.

Stock was offered to the general public at $20 per share in 1968, and within six months had soared to 60. Anyone who had invested $5,000 in fifty-cent shares was in a position to sell out at half a million dollars, and many of Nashville's most prominent citizens did just that.

Within a few months it became clear that competition was keen, expenses high, and sales far below expectations. The stock started on a long, sickening slide, falling to 2 late in 1969. The company changed its name to Performance Systems, Inc., and in February 1970 finally issued a financial report. In the first six months of 1969, it had suffered a loss of $5.5 million dollars. Of 1,600 franchises originally sold, only about two hundred were still operating. And the stock, now 2½, would trade in May as low as 5/16 (31 cents).

In mid-1970, Mr. Hooker, whose interests in the whole Minnie Pearl matter were under investigation by the SEC, was not only undiscouraged, but deep into his 1970 campaign re-running for governor. From all available polls, he was running ahead of his nearest opponent by more than two-to-one as election time neared, but he was not elected.

Many of these new issues were traded in the over-the-counter market, where manipulation was easier and controls more lax. Below are just a few examples of literally hundreds of such issues:

Stock	Date & Price	Offered	1971 Price	Percentage Decline
Datron System	9/02/69	8	1-7/8	77%
IMC International	10/08/69	8	2-3/4	45%
Computer Marketing	9/23/69	5	2	60%
Alpha Technology	9/04/69	3	3/8	87%
Compumedic	11/13/69	7	1	86%

I could cite many issues that had similar or worse performance. The "Over-the-Counter Securities Review," which keeps score, reports that in 1969 a total of 1,433 unlisted issues suffered price drops of 50% or more.

In mid-1968, National Student Marketing had been offered at $3 per share. In December, 1969, it reached a price of 70, which was 125 times earnings. By Spring of 1970, it was trading at a dollar.

The convalescent home industry was another that finally caught the fancy of the buying public in 1969. Speculators who put credence in the stories of fantastic earnings potentials of this industry regarded nursing home stocks as the easiest and quickest road to wealth. For a while they seemed to be right.

Four Seasons Nursing Centers was incorporated in 1967 following the combination of several companies engaged in the development, construction, management and operation of health care centers. During 1969, it was one of the most spectacular issues traded on the American Stock Exchange, selling as high as 90 3/4. Early in 1970, due in part to the general decline in the market and particularly to the weakness of issues in the franchising field, and in part to rumors that the company's earnings would be off, the shares sold down to 10. The SEC suspended trading in the stock at this point in order to investigate the validity of the company's projected earnings and solvency. On Monday, June 29, 1970, the company filed in federal court for reorganization under Chapter 10 of the National Bankruptcy Act.

Mutual Funds

Before 1960, mutual funds did not have too much bearing on the market's fluctuations. Since then, they have played an important role, and their influence on the market at times seems dangerous.

The mutual fund business by 1969 exhibited some characteristics of an overheated growth industry. Presumably this is because during the past three years great emphasis has been placed on performance. Hence, there was a great churning of portfolios, and often it seems that this is done without time for prudent judgment.

There are now approximately 750 mutual funds operating, totaling billions of dollars in assets and arranged in a seemingly endless variety of forms as dual purpose funds, hedge funds, special funds, performance funds .... In addition, there are other millions in investment trusts. Together, these funds account for over fifty percent of the trading on the New York Stock Exchange, and they are permitted to sell individual blocks of stock that individuals would otherwise have to register with the SEC. There is question as to whether such practice is equitable, as well as the extent to which it contributes to uncertainty and instability in our markets. One shudders to think what could happen if a majority of these funds turned decidedly bearish at the same time. In 1929 there were no giant mutual funds buying and selling enormous blocks of stock. In 1969 it was estimated that mutual funds alone held $37 billion of stocks, and had total assets of $50 billion.

At one time it seemed that mutual funds served a very helpful function, particularly to the small investor. But times have changed. In many cases, load (commission) charges are excessive, there is too much emphasis placed on performance, and – perhaps most important – there is too much money concentrated in the hands of a few people.

I have served as Chairman of the Board and a Director of a small mutual fund. But it is a *no load fund* (no sales commission) and has been kept small. The fund has done a great service for many small investors, such as retired people or school teachers, in the Princeton area. The mutual fund field as a whole, however, has grown much too fast, and some restrictive regulations are in order.

During the past two years, several so-called "hedge funds" have been organized, and have grown quite sizable. One authority states that more than 100 are in operation, managing several billions of dollars. Hedge funds are private pools of capital set up by a group of wealthy individuals; formed legally as a partnership, and with less than 100 stockholders, they are not subject to the jurisdiction and supervision of the Securities and Exchange Commission. The SEC is now conducting an investigation into the impact of these hedge funds on our markets.

Hedge funds can be in a long position in securities, they can go short, deal in puts and calls, purchase on margin, and not be responsible to any supervisory agency. Regular dividends are not paid, but at the year-end capital gains, if there are any, are distributed. Most of these funds are managed by young men in their thirties, referred to as the "go-go boys." They did not go through the difficult investment periods that periodically prevailed from 1920 to 1950. Many of them have only been in this business during the 1960-70 decade, and have been swept along in the current of a rampant speculation created in these years. They have somehow felt that stocks are always going to go up, with some corrections here and there. A close fraternity exists in this field, and if one "go-go boy" decides a certain stock is cheap, he at once gets his position. Then he whispers to one or two of his cronies and they do the same; before you know it, several funds are pouring millions of dollars into the stock, and it is run up to dizzy limits. Often the innocent investor is sucked in when he sees a certain stock suddenly become active and strong.

With these hedge funds, *performance* is the watchword. They are dangerous, and should not be allowed to function in their present form. The whole mutual fund field should be more carefully policed and restricted; and while the SEC is making an attempt to do this, it is woefully short of men and funds.

Although the SEC frowns upon "performance-fee" funds, their number has also grown rapidly in the past several years. As the name implies, these fund managers are paid on the basis of performance rather than the usual management fee. In other words, they must perform well in order to be paid a fee, and the better the performance the greater that fee becomes. A few of them are penalized for failure to perform. In these, the management company pays the fund a penalty for poor performance. However, many which were formed in 1968 and 1969 eliminated this feature, using only the bonus approach of the managers' earning extra money for superior performance. This one-sided approach particularly disturbs the SEC, a spokesman for which complains, "It's a 'heads I win, tails you lose' policy. And the loser is the investor."

According to an article in *Barron's*, March 2, 1970, there were only sixteen performance-fee funds in 1967; three years later, they numbered at least 145. A few are relatively small, but some run into the $200 million to $300 million category. The Oppenheimer Fund is close to $300 million, and Enterprise Fund over $800 million. At one point in 1970, Enterprise was enjoined by a Federal Court from selling its shares, following SEC charges that it had violated bookkeeping provisions of the Federal Securities Act.

Most of these funds go in heavily for glamor stocks and shares of smaller, little-known firms. This policy paid off handsomely in 1968, but backfired severely in 1969. Many of them sell short, buy restricted securities, trade in puts and calls and borrow money for leverage. Portfolio turnover is very high, ranging anywhere from 50% to 100%.

Realizing the size of these funds and that performance is their objective, it is easy to see how much influence they can bring to bear on the fluctuations of individual stocks and on the market generally. I cannot believe that they enhance the well-being of the stock market, contributing rather to its instability and speculative excesses.

In this chapter I have attempted to paint a picture of the action of the stock market in the 1960's. It is obvious that there was reckless speculation in addition to the solid growth reflected in certain companies' stocks. After 1967, volume on the New York Stock Exchange rose to heights not dreamed of a few years ago. There were many fifteen-million-share days, sometimes more, in the Sixties, which caught most New York Stock Exchange member firms without adequate help or equipment. Deliveries and confirmations became so delinquent that the SEC forced many firms to close certain of their branch offices, and to raise new capital. In fact, several well-known firms had to close their doors. This naturally caused anxiety among investors.

Even though New York Stock Exchange volume in 1969 reached nearly 3.3 billion, a number of the largest and most prominent brokerage firms reported losses in the millions for the year 1969.

With the lower volume characteristic of 1970 – and hence, lower profits for brokerage firms in general – several firms were forced to merge with others, and some closed their doors permanently. The low level of stock prices combined with the high cost of borrowing money put an unprecedented squeeze on their capital positions.

The following excerpts from "Rip Van Winkle Returns to Wall Street," an entertaining article published in March, 1969, by the well-known Investment Counselor David L. Babson, convey many of the decade's remarkable investment changes:[12]

"A bewildered Rip Van Winkle II returned to his Wall Street office this week after a twenty years' absence. Like his legendary ancestor of the Catskills, he had been presumed dead but actually had fallen into the same strange and prolonged sleep.

"His first surprise was the way people looked and dressed. The young men with long, flowing locks of hair who crowded the streets – were they reenacting the resurrection? And why were so many bare-thighed office girls dressed for tennis in the heart of the city?

"He wondered if the financial community had undergone similar drastic changes. He recalled that before he fell asleep, nearly all his cronies at banks, mutual funds and brokerage houses were waiting for the big postwar depression. 'Another 1929' was on everybody's mind. The main investment controversy was whether a 'prudent man' should have as much as 25% of his portfolio in common stocks.

"Few of his investor friends were then interested in common stock,

12. *Weekly Staff Letter.* Boston: David L. Babson & Co., Inc., March 27, 1969

which – as Rip recalled – were being appraised *at their lowest levels of the century*. General Motors and many other high-grade equities could be bought at dividend yields of 8-10%.

"As these memories rushed through his mind, Rip found himself in front of a familiar brokerage office. As he entered, he was appalled at the pandemonium inside – the deafening roar of voices, the constant jangle of telephones, the milling, carnival-like crowd. Could this be the same boardroom with its vast empty stillness – interrupted only by an occasional jiggle of the ticker – that he had visited, it seemed, only yesterday?

"Glancing at the posted Averages, Rip could not believe his eyes. Ever since he had started out on the Street in the mid-1930's, the Dow had ranged between 100 and 200. On his last day of work in 1949, it was a lofty 176. What was this 900 figure? Had the Average been subjected to a 'reverse split'?

"Rip shouldered his way to the broad tape just in time to catch the latest bond quotes. One of his favorite issues was the bellwether Union Pacific 2-1/2s of 1991, which sold at 96 on that fateful day in 1949. Only 56? And Rip sensed that the 40-point drop must be only part of the real investment loss if the prices of hamburgers and haircuts were a measure of what had happened to the dollar's value.

"Spying a life-long acquaintance at one of the desks, he started elbowing a path towards him. Old Wintergreen, Rip thought, still has that same knowing look about him. He sure never fell for all that 'growth stock' malarkey. Better find out what's going on from him.

"After the two friends exchanged greetings and Rip related the details of his misadventure, the conversation went something like this:

Rip: I can hardly believe the changes I've seen. What are you telling your customers to do these days?

Wintergreen: Well, as you know, Rip, I never buck the trend. The things to buy now are stocks with exciting futures – nursing home chains, highway franchisers, anti-pollution firms, computer services, oceanography.

Rip: I don't know what you are talking about, but I suppose these are the stocks that give the highest yields now. You were always keen on the big dividend-payers like Telephone and Big Steel.

Wintergreen: That idea is long dead. No one is interested in dividends any more. You do far better by going for capital growth. So you look for companies whose earnings are jumping 20%, 30%, even 50% a year.

Rip: I remember once you told me never to pay over 12 times earnings for *any* stock. I expect that a wise old bird like you is still picking them up for a song.

Wintergreen: Times have changed, Rip. You have to be aggressive today. People are paying 40, 60, even 100 times earnings, but it's worth it to get into these dynamic new businesses.

Rip: You're confusing me. I thought you didn't believe in growth stocks.

Wintergreen: Well, I missed out on Eastman Kodak, Corning Glass and Merck, but a few years ago I decided to catch up by buying tomorrow's growth stocks.

Rip: But what about bonds? You used to say they would be the buy of a lifetime if yields got up over 3%.

Wintergreen: You can pick up Treasuries at 6¼ and corporates at 7½%. In fact, Transcontinental Gas Pipe Line is just bringing out a new debenture to yield well over 8%. But nobody wants bonds with inflation eating up income and principal at 4-5% a year.

Rip: Then you've changed your mind about bonds, too?

Wintergreen: Rip, you'd better get back to your office and let the boys over there bring you up to date.

"As his partner's secretary guided him down the office corridor, almost all the men he noticed – even those in private offices with titles on the door – seemed to be in their 20's or early 30's. He recalled that back in the late 1940's, most of the people in the business were in their 50's and 60's, and almost no one was under 40.

"His old associate was, of course, overjoyed to see him. After the strange tale was told, he was asked about his most immediate needs. 'The first thing I want,' Rip said, 'is a summary-type report showing how the major economic and investment benchmarks have changed while I've been gone.'

Office Memo to Rip Van Winkle II

	March 1949	March 1969	% Change
Economic Yardsticks			
Population (mil.)	149	202	+ 36%
Gross National Product (bil.)	$259	$903	+248
Industrial Output (index)	66	170	+157
Value of the Dollar	$1.00	$0.67	-33

Dow-Jones Industrial Average			
Price	176	917	+420
Earnings	$23	$60	+160
Dividends	$12	$31	+160
Investment Appraisals			
Common Stocks			
Price-Earnings Ratios*	8x	15x	+ 90
Dividend Yields*	6.8%	3.4%	- 50
Bond Yields			
Treasury Bills	1.00%	5.95%	+495
Long-Term Treasuries	2.40%	6.25%	+160
Single-A Corporates	2.90%	7.05%	+140
High-Grade Municipals	2.20%	5.35%	+140

*Dow-Jones Industrial

As he studied the memo item by item, Rip was astonished at the enormous growth of the economy during his absence. The 'consensus' of the late 1940's had certainly been dead wrong about the future. And the value of the dollar, far from increasing, had shrunk by a third.

"What surprised him the most, however, was the complete turnabout of investment appraisals. He noted that while stocks yielded two-and-a-half times as much as bonds in 1949, bonds now yielded over twice as much as stocks.

"Even more amazing was how effective common stocks had been as investments during the 20-year span. The Dow Average had quintupled. True, half its advance was due to the increase in its price-earnings ratio. But the fact that its earnings and dividends had both risen by 160% was particularly impressive.

"Rip also noted that the Dow was currently being appraised at 15 times earnings. This was in marked contrast to the fantastic multiples on 'tomorrow's growth stocks' his friend Wintergreen thought were so attractive. Here at last was one thing that had not really changed much at all."

CHAPTER SIX

INFLATION

On September 23, 1969, *The New York Times* published the following editorial on "The Shrinking Dollar," reproduced below:

"Yesterday's report on consumer prices indicates that inflation is still cutting into the buying power of the family dollar at an annual rate of roughly a nickel. The continued upsurge in living costs makes graphic how little restraining effect has yet been exerted by monetary policies so tight that the Federal Government itself has to pay annual interest of 8 per cent to borrow money for a year and a half.

"Washington has had to face no comparable rates since 1859, when the nation was on the eve of the Civil War and investors had every reason to question whether they would ever be repaid. The Federal Government is not alone in being forced to pay what by all earlier standards in this century must be regarded as exorbitant rates. Recently, to borrow funds for six months, New York City had to pay almost 7.5 per cent in interest on tax-exempt notes, a return equivalent to 15 per cent interest for persons in the 50 per cent tax bracket. Some major, well-known corporations have been able to sell bonds only by paying 9 per cent or more. Meanwhile, the small saver is confined to savings bank interest of roughly 5 per cent, a return that barely matches inflation's erosion of the dollar.

"Thus far the Federal Reserve Board's credit restrictions and the Government's 10 per cent income tax surcharge – both aimed at the same objective – have failed to stem one of the most virulent inflations in the nation's peacetime history. The increases just announced in 1970 automobile model prices combine with the August figures on consumer prices to demonstrate how elusive stability remains in the face of extraordinarily restrictive fiscal and monetary policy.

"By now the inflation has proceeded so long and so far that the expectation of continuing rapid inflation is a key factor fueling the bonfire. For many skeptics about the adequacy of the Administration's program, the temptation becomes overwhelming to borrow at any interest rate.

"The economic astrologers are divided in their forecasts, and those who draw up economic horoscopes for the Nixon Administration are seeking to assure the public that if it has patience the boom will break in time, inflation will taper off to 3 or 4 per cent annually and something will be left of the dollar. But the ordinary citizen sees around him daily a spiraling race between wages and prices, and if he is a pensioner, a small saver or is living on a fixed income, he has felt very personally the inroads of inflation.

"On that basis many Americans are likely to accept with extreme reserve the assurance given again yesterday at the White House that the Administration's anti-inflation measures are beginning to take hold.

"There is further proof of the ravages of inflation. As dramatic as was the intensity of the inflation spiral last month (February) in the face of credit restraint, high interest rates, and high taxes, the havoc played with the purchasing power of the dollar is a fresh warning to investors. In a single year, the value of the pre-World War II 1939 dollar has dropped almost two cents, or from 40.5 cents in March 1968 to 38.6 cents in March 1969. Since the beginning of the unparalleled long business boom in December, 1960, the value of the 1939 dollar has fallen almost 18% from 46.9 cents to 38.6 cents."[13]

From *The Wall Street Journal,* also early in 1969: "The most widely followed fever chart of inflation is the index of prices paid by consumers – the so-called 'Cost of Living' index. The measure of inflation's pace, year to year, is the annual rate of increase in this index. The table below traces the annual rates of increase in the consumer price index through the current decade. The figure for 1969 is the annual rate of gain recorded in the first ten months of the year.

Year	% Gain	Year	% Gain
1960	1.6	1965	2.0
1961	0.6	1966	3.3
1962	1.2	1967	3
1963	1.7	1968	4.6
1964	1.1	1969	5.9

"Two things are evident at a glance. First, the climb in the price level during the first half of the decade was negligible. Second, the

13. *The New York Times* Sept. 23, 1969, Editorial.
Used by permission.

fastest-tempo rise has actually occurred since official efforts to 'cool things off' began."[14]

People now are asking, will inflation really be curbed? Will a recession develop? If so, how severe? There are many reasons for this frightening inflationary trend: the terrific cost of the Vietnam War, the colossal amounts of money spent on our space program, and foreign aid and vast sums expended by the government on its many other projects. Another potent factor has been the growing amount of spendable income in the hands of the majority of Americans, coupled in many instances with a scarcity of goods.

The increase in the cost of labor is bound to rise with the increase in the consumer price index, but the table below on the subject reveals some interesting figures. *The Wall Street Journal* goes on to comment: "The recent runaway in the 'Cost of People' has been pretty well publicized. But a quick look at the rise in total wage and salary payments in the economy, compared with what has happened to corporate profits, helps put the picture in perspective. This table covers the last half-decade. Figures in both salary-wage and profit columns represent billions. The 1969 figures are current annual rates.

Year	Salaries, Wages	Corporate Profits
1965	$358	$46
1966	$394	$49
1967	$423	$47
1968	$465	$49
1969	$513	$51

What these two columns add up to is this: Wage and salary payments, now roaring along well above the half-a-trillion dollars level, are up some 43% just since 1965, while corporate profits are up only about 11%."[15]

Mention of recent significant wage increases should include the Pan American Airways settlement of 37.4% for a three year period as well as the New York City subway workers' $120 million, called "staggering" by John T. Rowan, President of the Manhattan Transit Authority. Similar increases are taking place regularly, in the building industry particularly.

---

14. *The Wall Street Journal,* December 1, 1969

15. *The Wall Street Journal,* September 15, 1969

In *The Wall Street Journal* dated July 28, 1969, Labor Secretary Willard Schultz was quoted as saying, "Labor contracts with inflationary increases in wages and benefits over a period of years could spell trouble for business and labor when the economy cools." He announced that contracts settled in the first half of 1969 provided median increases of 7.1% a year, up from 6% for all of the preceding year.

An article appearing in the "First National City Monthly Letter" states, "Since late 1965 wages and fringes have increased at an annual rate of more than 7%, well above the nearly 4% average rate of increase in consumer prices. Real compensation per man hour for the average worker has risen at the rate of 3.4%. Meanwhile, the increases per man hour slowed to an average 2.5% rate. This means that labor's share in total income has recovered most of the dip in the early sixties."[16]

A well known financial paper contained these frightening remarks concerning construction costs in New York City: "Construction costs are already so high in this city that unsubsidized apartments can be built only for the rich. The community must underwrite new housing for hundreds of thousands of New Yorkers through low-rent projects or tax subsidies to middle-income units. The high price of building is one reason why low-income families seeking admission to municipal housing would have to wait a full half-century under current construction schedules.

"But the present costs will appear modest when the public has to start paying for the new union agreements in process of being signed by construction labor and management here. The pattern calls for increases in wage and fringe benefits ranging from 35 to 40 per cent over a three-year term.

"And even these fantastic jumps in pay scales, already among the highest in any blue-collar field, are being rejected by the union representing sheet metal workers and steamfitters. They have called strikes for more money. An element in the sheet metal walkout is union resistance to an employer demand for a cut in the industry's staggering overtime bill – a cut that would not only reduce costs but would also open more job opportunities for Negroes and Puerto Ricans in this lily-white trade.

"The extortionate settlements being made in New York are in line with those being won by construction unions all over the country, keeping intact their record for outpacing all other unions in the

16. *The First National City Monthly*, July, 1969

insatiability of their demands. Collusive relationships with their contractors and a long history of restrictive practices on productivity and membership, backed up by political alliances and building codes that defeat the public interest, have given the construction trades an immunity from the restraints that supposedly operate in a competitive economy.

"They roll on serenely, confident that the nationwide shortage of housing and the still brisk demand for new office and industrial facilities will keep their monopoly unbroken and their tightly controlled membership fully employed. Federal, state and local governments could use their counterstrength as major participants in construction contracts, but neither political party is ready to take the risk of alienating these A.F.L.–C.I.O. power centers. So the war against inflation is put in the deep freeze and the dollar suffers another blow."

An article from the "First National City Monthly Letter," July 1969, reads: "Taking account of both severity and duration, the inflation of the past three years is the worst since the late Forties. Although there has been some talk of wage and price controls, these proposals have received little serious consideration – in distinct contrast to previous wartime periods. Congress and the public appear willing to allow the price of labor as well as the prices of most goods to be determined in the marketplace. One reason may be the lack of broad public support for the Vietnam War. Another is the lesson learned from World War II and the Korean War – that price and wage controls have only limited and transitory effectiveness. They inevitably break down under an accumulation of imbalances. Moreover, the present inflation is largely the product of excessive monetary and fiscal expansion over the past several years. Only through monetary and fiscal restraint can we attack inflation at its source."[17]

On June 12, 1970, *The New York Times* carried the following comments regarding the views of T. Rowe Price, renowned Baltimore mutual fund manager, about inflation:

"In his view, the Full Employment Act of 1946 requires that nearly everyone work even if inflation is a direct result – and that is the inevitable result of full employment.

"He believes that the masses who elect the President and members of Congress will not support any Government in the near future that puts the control of inflation ahead of full employment and continued prosperity.

---

17. *The First National City Monthly,* July, 1969

"Uncontrolled inflation will therefore result," ' and, Mr. Price says, '"uncontrolled inflation has always led to a boom and bust."[18]

Labor costs will keep rising – unions are not likely to be stripped of their favored position in collective bargaining, which is at the root of the national pay increases now running at about 7%.

For the past twenty years, William McChesney Martin, the able, courageous St. Louis banker, has been Chairman of the Federal Reserve Board. His insistence on conservative policies has been opposed by Presidents, Congressmen, and even some of his associates. But he has stood firm.

Martin retired on February 1, 1970. President Nixon gave him a farewell White House dinner, attended by many dignitaries. His parting remark to the President and guests was, "I leave behind, unsolved, the worst inflation since the Civil War."

A 1970 Harris poll revealed that 60% of all families felt that between inflation and taxes they were worse off that year than the last. Adding to their frustration the declining stock market, and to the entire scene the discontent of the blacks and the young generation, it is hard to find any part of the country which is not deeply disturbed about some major aspect of our national life.

Along this line, it is interesting to go back to President Johnson's State of the Union address in January 1968, when in his opening remarks he said, "There is in this land a certain restlessness – a questioning." Later on, he asked, "Why, then, this restlessness when the nation is wealthier than ever before in terms of Gross National Product, higher pay checks, and seventy million T.V. sets?"

President Johnson failed to realize that the bewilderment and frustration of our people is not over material things but over our policies, purposes, priorities, and fundamental moral questions.

---

18. *The New York Times*, June 12, 1970

CHAPTER SEVEN

MONEY RATES AND THE BOND MARKET

There were obviously many upheavals in the 1960-70 decade – in the stock market, in interest rates, in our ghettoes, in wage levels, in our colleges and universities. But the one upheaval probably least understood, and the one that has received the least publicity, has been the one in interest rates, or the rising cost of money.

At the start of 1960, the yield on long-term government bonds was 4½%, but during the year this yield went as low as 3½% and did not reach a 4% level again until the beginning of 1962. During the entire year of 1962, and for most of 1963, the yield held fairly steady at 4%. For the most part, it remained a little under 4% during 1964. By the end of 1965 it was at 4½% again, and did not fluctuate much during the year. But from this point on, bond prices started a steady decline, and at the end of 1966 the yield was 5½%. By the end of 1969, it was 7%, and in February 1970, the yield on the 4's of 1980 reached 7.6%.

I might add here that, along with many others, I misjudged the bond market. In November 1967, when Standard Oil of New Jersey offered a long term 6% bond at par, I recommended it at the offering price of 100 to all of my institutional accounts holding excess cash that could be put in bonds. Initially, the bonds went to a premium of 105 ($1050 each), but by late 1970 were selling at 78 ($780) to yield well over 8½% to maturity. I have followed the course of buying additional bonds to average down the cost, but this illustrates what a drastic change has taken place in our money markets.

What brought about this precipitous rise in money rates? Our balance of payments figures were steadily worsening. We were losing gold at a rapid rate, and were attempting to fight the longest and costliest war in history without increasing taxes or instituting wartime controls.

In the autumn of 1965, Chairman of the Federal Reserve Board William McChesney Martin felt that we must take appropriate action, and urged his associates to raise the rediscount rate in order to make it more difficult to borrow money. He went directly to President Johnson with his recommendation, but the President was unalterably opposed to it. Johnson wanted to prove to the nation that we could have guns and butter and still be able to borrow money at a low rate. However, Chairman Martin was adamant, and raised the rediscount rate from 4% to 4½% on December 5, 1965. Our bond markets reacted by beginning their long slide, eventually declining in a chaotic state. By 1970, yields of as high as 11% could be secured on sound corporate obligations and as high as 7½% on sound tax-exempt bonds. On the week of February 3, 1970, our government paid the highest interest rate on short-term obligations since the Civil War:

8-1/4% notes due August 15, 1971;
8-1/8% notes due August 15, 1973;
8% notes due August 15, 1977.

The table below appeared in the "First National City Monthly Letter" of December, 1969.[19] It depicts industrial bond yields and depreciation of money for 1967, 1968, and 1969 in five nations, including the United States:

Industrial Bond Yields*	United Kingdom	Canada	United States	France	Germany (Fed. Rep.)
Oct 67	7.64%	7.50%	6.06%	6.25%	6.50%
Oct 68	8.39	7.50	6.54 †	6.88	6.38
Oct 69	10.52	8.90	8.05 †	8.00	7.50
Change 67-69	2.88	1.40	1.99	1.75	1.00
Depreciation of Money**					
Oct 67	1.9%	3.5%	2.5%	3.10%	1.1%
Oct 68	5.3	4.0	4.4	5.3	2.2
Sep 69	4.9	4.3	5.3***	5.7	2.7

---

*Based on industrial bond yields as of end of October except for Canada, which are as of November 10.

† Weighted average yields on new AAA corporate issues.

**As measured inversely by increases in consumer price indexes during the 12 months ended on dates shown.

***October.

19 *The First National City Monthly*, December, 1969

An interesting observation is that at the end of 1969, the dividend yield on the thirty stocks composing the Dow-Jones Industrial Average was approximately 4% – but an investor could get from 8% to 10% on corporate bonds. This was quite a spread, and if one chose to buy deep discount bonds, such as Standard Oil of New Jersey 6's of 1997 at 78, his yield was a comfortable 8½% to maturity. This was twice the yield on most common stocks – and with an assurance of twenty-two points' appreciation. These two advantages certainly afforded the investor some protection against inflation. Or, if an investor wanted an earlier maturity, he could buy A. T. & T.'s 2¾% bonds due in 1975 at about 77. At that price the "yield to maturity" is 7.85%. Since the bonds will be paid off in 1975 at 100, the investor is assured an appreciation of nearly 30%. This, of course, is reflected in the 7.85 *yield to maturity.*

For the past twenty years, most investors have ignored bonds. Yields were low; common stocks offered almost as much return, in addition to possible capital appreciation. But there has been a radical change in conditions, and by 1969-70, more and more money was finding its way into bonds.

U. S. Treasury 4¼'s 1987-92

These bonds were offered in August, 1962, at par. In 1919, under the Second Liberty Bond Act, Congress had authorized a 4¼% limit on the interest rate of the long-term government obligations issued under that section. Later on, the Act was amended, authorizing the Treasury to issue other obligations called "notes," which matured in not less than one year or more than five years (subsequently changed to seven). It could also issue obligations called "bills" with maturities of not more than one year. This action proved to be a near-fatal mistake, because since then, all government financing has had to be done with short maturities. As shown above, our government recently had to pay 8-1/4% for bonds maturing August 15, 1971.

But the 4-1/4's of 1987-92 are interesting for another feature. *They can be used at par to pay federal inheritance taxes.* (There are several government issues carrying this same privilege. Your banker, broker or Investment Counselor will gladly furnish a complete list.) Incidentally, this privilege is printed on the face of the bond so that it cannot be changed. In the Spring of 1970, these bonds were selling at about 65, to yield nearly 7.4% to maturity. A year later they were trading at 79.

I have many clients who are seventy years old or more. Any individual of seventy years whose estate will face a sizable inheritance tax should buy enough of these bonds to cover it. Many of my readers may not realize that this opportunity exists, but it is obviously a big saving. All of my clients aged seventy or more own them.

Four or five years ago, Helen and I were spending the night at the Barclay Hotel in Philadelphia. We went into the popular cocktail room prior to dinner. As usual, the room was well filled, and we were seated close to two very well-dressed mesdames. They were discussing their investments, and we clearly heard one say, "This has been a terrible year. I was advised to take my money from the savings bank at 3½% and buy the new "E" 3¾'s. Soon I was told to cash them in and go into the savings and loan at 4½%. I had just done this when the government issued 5% notes. Today I was told that Philadelphia Electric is about to issue 5 3/8% bonds. Why can't they make up their minds?"

Many times since I have wondered how she felt by 1970, when one could get 11% on good corporate bonds, 7½% on sound tax exempts, and 8¼% on government notes maturing in one year. I am afraid that she would be unhappy and completely frustrated.

The second lady, I remember, had remained silent about bonds, but later commented, "Well, I certainly am not going to buy stocks as my broker advised. I said to him, 'If stocks are so cheap, why are there always so many of them for sale?' He couldn't explain that . . . ."

CHAPTER EIGHT

MEN ON THE MOON

1969 is a year that will long be remembered for an adventure sufficiently fantastic and incredible to eclipse any previous accomplishment in the history of mankind – when Apollo 11 first put man on the moon. Captain Neil Armstrong was the first man to set foot on lunar soil, at 10:56:20 p.m. July 20, 1969. He had the feeling that the earth would never be the same again. Soon followed onto the moon by his fellow astronaut, Armstrong and Colonel Edwin Aldrin, Jr. spent about twenty-one hours at a landing spot called Tranquility Base. It was a desolate plain of rocks and dust. Maximum distance from the earth – 252,710 miles.

Nearly as breathtaking as the actual landing was the fact that anyone on earth with a television set could witness this incredible feat unfolding step by step.

On July 21, 1969, *The New York Times* carried a clever ad of Gimbel's Department Store entitled, "Ever since Adam and Eve":

> Said Adam to Eve
> "I believe I perceive
> the face of the man on the moon."
>
> Said Eve, "We could fly to the
> guy and say 'hi'
> If you would just invent the balloon."
>
> Today goes to show
> How a nation can grow
> When two people gaze at the moon.
>
> We broke Newton's law
> And the world saw with awe
> the face of our man on the moon.[20]

An equally successful second landing on the moon occurred in December, 1969, with astronauts Al Bean and Charles Conrad. They

20. *The New York Times*, July 21, 1969

landed Apollo 12 at a place named "The Sea of Storms," and had more time than lunar predecessors to explore, set up experiments, and collect more and bigger rocks. The landing area had a thicker cover of dust and the soil was lighter than that of Tranquility Base.

Within thirteen months, the impressive Apollo flights 13 and 14 had immortalized the additional names of Roosa, Mitchell and Shepard, and Swigert, Lovell and Haise. Later flight No. 15 followed with Scott, Irwin and Worden.

Groundwork for these flights had been painstakingly laid during the Sixties. President John F. Kennedy, in his inaugural address in 1961, had urged an aggressive space campaign. John H. Glenn's famous three orbits around the earth had been made in 1962, and in December, 1968, Apollo 8 had circled the moon ten times with astronauts James A. Lovell, Jr., Frank Borman, and William A. Anders.

All of these missions were accomplished with precision. The only accident to mar this perfect record occurred in January, 1967, when astronauts Gus Grissom, Ed White, and Roger Chaffee – three valiant and intrepid men – were burned to death in an explosion that took place in a training spacecraft at Cape Kennedy. The nation mourned this tragedy.

That all of these remarkable feats were accomplished in an eight-year period is nothing short of phenomenal. What has all of this cost in dollars? I doubt if there are accurate figures on the amount of money spent by NASA. We do know it is several billion. There are many who opposed such huge expenditures at a time when we had critical domestic problems crying to be solved. Author Norman Mailer posed the question: "Was the Apollo 11 venture the greatest technological achievement of our time, in fact a step forward – or was it civilized man's most profound mistake?" There were many who felt that this fantastic accomplishment was worth all it cost, and will eventually lead to the solution of many scientific mysteries.

On July 26, 1969, *The Wall Street Journal* carried an editorial on the Apollo achievement, beautifully capsulizing the pros and cons of the argument:

"For the past eight days the world has thrilled to the Apollo mission, now safely accomplished. The moon landing, whatever doubts about it linger, has injected a sense of achievement into a species of late notably bereft of that gift.

"Conquest of the moon comes at a time when man has come to doubt his ability to affect his own future. Seldom if ever have so many of his problems seemed beyond his ken. The ancient threat of war has evolved into a threat of extinction. Pestilence and famine have yielded considerably to human control, only to raise the new perplexity of overpopulation. Economic abundance, in those nations that have won it, seems on the surface only to breed social breakdown. Bewildered by such paradox, man starts to sense that he has lost control, that events are shaped by some capricious if not malevolent teleology.

"In Apollo we can find new hope that this is not so. Even detractors of the space program must admire it as a beautiful demonstration of human energy and talent. There is something vastly inspiring in the sheer achievement. Less than 10 years ago men decided to put their stamp on the moon. Today it is done with spectacular competence.

"Splendid as it is, the Apollo achievement must be kept in perspective. It is particularly foolish to assume that if man can go to the moon he ought to be able to solve his problems on earth. A great deal of the political reasoning behind the space effort specifically concerned instilling a sense of national achievement. From the range of goals that might have served this purpose the moon mission was selected because it was both dramatic and feasible. Man decided to go to the moon precisely because it was something he could do.

"Through history, indeed, man has been relatively successful in mastering the elements. He could outwit other animals in finding food, capture the fire that threatened, turn the floods of the Nile to his own ends, use the winds to sail the seas, harness the energy of coal, oil and steam, fly the skies and split the atom. Now he can walk on the moon.

"Besides all this, man has struggled with more limited success to master himself. From the cave family to the nation-state, he has tried to find a social organism to contain and direct his vision and greed, his love and hate, his wisdom and folly. So today our real problems – whether war or slums or race or even environmental pollution – are not mainly problems of technology but of social and economic organization. They are not the easy problems of mastering the elements, but the hard problems of mastering man.

"The space program can be faulted for turning energy and talent from the hard problems to easier ones. Still, one can also doubt that the problems here on earth will yield to material inputs in any decisive way. Perhaps they will yield as much as anything to a touch of inspiration, a dollop of confidence in man's abilities.

"Therein may lie the human meaning of the mission that ended with its Pacific splashdown yesterday. That man can walk on the moon does not prove he can do everything, but it does prove he can still do something. In that there is a measure of hope for a doubting age."[21]

21. *The Wall Street Journal,* July 26, 1969

CHAPTER NINE

THE NIXON ADMINISTRATION

In March of 1968, President Lyndon Baines Johnson appeared on a national television hookup. At the end of his address he amazed the nation by saying, "I shall not seek and will not accept the nomination of my party."

By this time we were more deeply involved in Vietnam than ever. President Johnson was receiving a rising crescendo of criticism, not only from Republicans but from prominent members of his own party. It appeared that even Secretary of Defense Robert McNamara had joined the opposition, because he suddenly resigned to accept the presidency of the World Bank. In speaking of our predicament, author J. B. Priestley said, "A great country based on a noble revolutionary idea is now tearing itself apart, and may experience more anger, violence, shame and sorrow before it can heal itself."

One of President Johnson's most severe and effective critics was Democratic Senator Eugene McCarthy of Minnesota. He had announced before Johnson's withdrawal that he would be a candidate for the Presidency. Entering the primary election in New Hampshire, he had won the majority of delegates. Shortly before Johnson made his pronouncement, Senator Robert Kennedy of New York had made public his candidacy as well.

We are all familiar with the events of the 1968 campaign: Robert Kennedy's brutal assassination in Los Angeles in June, the disgraceful and humiliating Democratic convention in Chicago, and finally the nomination of Hubert H. Humphrey as the Democratic candidate. Several weeks earlier the Republicans had met in Miami and had nominated Richard Milhous Nixon. He surprised his followers and the nation at large by choosing Spiro Agnew, Governor of Maryland, as his running mate.

Richard Nixon had been narrowly defeated for the Presidency in 1960 by John Kennedy. In 1962 he was thoroughly beaten for the Governorship of California, at which time he not-too-prophetically declared to newspaper reporters in Los Angeles, "This is my last press conference." But he managed to fight off his bitterness and by 1965 started to fashion the campaign that would eventually lead him to the

White House. He stumped for any Republican who needed his help. He was wise enough to court Southern Republican leaders, such as Strom Thurmond, knowing that he would have to carry some Southern states to win the Republican nomination and the Presidency. Subsequent events proved him to be absolutely right, for he lost the large Eastern states of New York, Pennsylvania, and Massachusetts. Without this help from the South, Humphrey could have beaten him.

Nixon's rating with the public following his election gradually rose. One of his first steps was to promise the deescalation of the war in Vietnam, by means of gradual troop withdrawal. At the same time, he utilized the direct approach via television to quiet the critics of Vietnam and at least temporarily put a halt to demonstrations and peace marches.

It soon became clear that President Nixon intended to relegate to the background the Great Society ventures of L. B. J., directing national attention instead to the total American "environment" or "quality of life." This meant that the Nixon Administration would bypass L. B. J.'s programs in favor of distributing federal funds over a much broader area and to a larger set of beneficiaries. The Johnson Administration emphasized help to the needy blacks and ghettoes of the larger cities. Nixon, on the other hand, seems bent on concentrating on the wants of the "great silent white majority," in suburban areas as well as in the cities.

In a speech to the nation's governors in December, 1969, he said it is time "to move forward on the whole subject of the quality of life in America, the environment, how we can clean up our rivers and our water, our air and our streets and our cities – how we can move forward on all fronts."

Naturally, there are many who do not agree with President Nixon's policies, both Democrats and Republicans. One of his severest Republican critics is John W. Gardner, former Secretary of Health, Education and Welfare. Until December 9, 1969, he had refrained from public criticism of the Nixon Administration. But on this day, in a speech to the National Press Club in Washington, he delivered a strong indictment of leadership at various levels, and bore down particularly hard on the Presidency. Throughout the nation, he said, there is a deep and pervasive feeling among all segments of the populace that things aren't working. "When the great majority of Americans share that uneasiness, when a growing number are losing all confidence in our society, when the problems themselves are terrifyingly real, then it is immoral for our National leaders in the Congress and the Executive branch to temporize. It is indecent for them to let us imagine that we can solve our problems without money or that we can afford to tackle them. Only the President's clearly expressed concern and clearly stated priorities can mobilize the Federal apparatus, encourage Congress to shake off its lethargy, and enable leaders in other sectors of American life to move decisively."

For some time Mr. Gardner had felt that the White House seemed to concentrate its greatest lobbying efforts in Congress on matters such as winning approval for the antiballistic missile system or the appointment of Judge Clement F. Haynsworth, Jr., to the Supreme Court.

In conclusion Mr. Gardner said, "We know what our problems are, but seem incapable of summoning our will and resources to act. We are seized by a kind of paralysis of the will. It is like a waking nightmare."

The alarms sounded in 1968 by the Kerner Commission and the Eisenhower Commission about the drift toward racist division, repression, and rebellion were heard but apparently not heeded. Our National Security Council still deals with foreign affairs, not domestic ones, and the Nixon Administration has not discovered the key to opening fruitful discussions with the nation's Negro community.

On August 3, 1969, James Reston, in his column in *The New York Times,* had this to say: "President Nixon must know that he is dramatizing the secondary questions and using them to avoid the primary questions. His main problems lie with the budget, with taxes, with the races, with peace in Vietnam, with the Russians, and disarmament, but he has not really been dealing with them. He has been concentrating on politics and publicity and the main policy questions will still face him under more difficult circumstances."[22]

Many of us feel that one of our greatest problems today is that of assimilating the Negroes into our society. If we fail to solve this problem, we will continue to have race riots and civil disturbances rock the nation. In the face of this, President Nixon not only has failed to find the key to talking with them and improving their plight, but seems to be going out of his way to antagonize them and drive them farther and farther away from any hopeful pacification.

On February 19, 1970, Tom Wicker of *The New York Times* wrote a profound column on the death of integration which went to the heart of the problem. Among other things, he concluded, "The Senate of the United States has now cravenly abandoned the policy of racial integration – sixteen years after it was born in a Supreme Court

22. James Reston in *The New York Times,* August 3, 1969. Used by permission.

decision, ninety-four years after the Civil War, Reconstruction ended in a similar sellout, and less than a week after President Nixon, on Lincoln's Birthday, gave the signal of surrender."[23]

Wicker maintained that this legislation was exactly what the Southern segregationists had wanted. "That is what their ally in the White House is willing to permit. That is what their dupes in the Senate have approved."[24] He went on to point out that for eighty years the nation simply defaulted until it became clear that the almost forgotten Civil War debt had to be paid, paid in full and without any more stalling.

"That is clearer than ever, because we are not dealing in 1970 with five million ignorant field hands in the cotton South, as we were in 1876. But once again, the Union is defaulting; once again, its capacity to pay has been found grievously wanting; and still its moral resources are sadly undeveloped. Poor old Union! Its great and generous dreams falling one by one to dusty death."[25]

Early in 1970, former Governor of Alabama George C. Wallace announced that he would not run for the Presidency in 1972 because of President Nixon's stand on segregation. As we all know, Mr. Wallace is one of the nation's most rabid racists. It looks more than ever as though President Nixon has completely surrendered to the racist elements of the South – and for what purpose? To strengthen the Republican party's chances of winning the 1972 election? Time and events will tell.

---

23. Tom Wicker in *The New York Times,* February 19, 1970. Used by permission.

24. *Ibid.*

25. *Ibid.*

CHAPTER TEN

PRINCETON

I have now lived in Princeton twenty-five years, and I can say truthfully that they have been the most rewarding and fascinating years of my life. Princeton is a beautiful and delightful little city as well as a wealthy one, and was only a country town twenty-five years ago. Enriched with natural beauty and influenced to a great extent by the university atmosphere, it possesses great culture in addition to its charm. During the years, I have been fortunate enough to meet and become closely acquainted with some members of the faculty known nationally and internationally. Time and space will not permit the mention of many, but there are two men who deserve special comment.

Soon after joining the Nassau Club I was made Treasurer and a member of the Board of Trustees; in 1953 I was elected President. Princeton has always been, and still is, a little insular. To put it another way, a non-Princeton graduate has one strike against him in competing with Princeton men. My election to the presidency of the Nassau Club was especially satisfying, because I believe I was the first man elected to that office who was either not a Princeton graduate or had not been on the faculty.

EDWIN S. CORWIN
1878 – 1963

During the several years that I served in these offices, I came to know well some very interesting men. One of them was Dr. Edwin S. Corwin, who had been chosen by Woodrow Wilson to succeed him as the Head of Princeton's Woodrow Wilson School of International Affairs.

Ed Corwin was one of the most fascinating men I have met. Short in stature, he was quite distinguished-looking, with gray hair, fine features, and sparkling, mischievous blue eyes. Over the years we became good friends.

When I first met him, he was about seventy, and had retired from the faculty five years earlier. He was extremely active, and since he had established a world-wide reputation as the leading authority on international and Constitutional law, he was in constant demand to appear before important audiences across the nation and abroad. *The New York Times* quoted him frequently on questions of jurisprudence.

One could write an entire book about this man, but one anecdote must serve to depict something of the high esteem in which he was held.

Helen and I met Ed and his wife in the Nassau Club lounge one evening. As usual, he was as chipper as a cricket (now about eighty years old), but his voice was quite hoarse. I inquired, "Ed, do you have bronchitis?"

"No, Harland," he replied, "I have been talking too damned much. Last week I lectured in Seattle, San Francisco and Los Angeles on three successive days and it was too much. My doctor tells me that I must rest for at least a month."

Continuing, he said, "You know, Foster Dulles called me yesterday and said, 'Ed, we're having a very important gathering in Washington next week and we want you to attend so that we can have the benefit of your advice.' Foster said that Anthony Eden, Adenauer and the Premiers of the Five Powers would be there. You know what I told Foster, Harland? 'I have a bad throat and can't come. If they want to see me, it will have to be in Princeton.' " I learned later that they all did come to Princeton, and spent the day in conference with him.

Ed died in 1963 at the age of eight-five, and his wife passed away recently at ninety-two. A few of his major contributions as a teacher, author, lecturer and consultant are listed below. To attempt to recite all of his accomplishments would require many pages.

He authored many books, of which some of the more important were:

John Marshall and the Constitution – 1919
The Constitution and What It Means Today – 1920
The Twilight of the Supreme Court – 1934
The President of the U. S.: Office and Powers – 1940
Total War and the Constitution – 1947

Other significant honors included:

Adviser to the PWA on Constitutional questions, 1935;
Special Assistant to the Attorney General of the United States, 1936;
Recipient of the Franklin Medal, American Philosophical Society, 1940;
Recipient of the Henry N. Phillips Prize in the Science and Philosophy of Jurisprudence, 1942.

The original building that housed the Woodrow Wilson School faced Washington Road at Prospect Street. It was a lovely brick building, but in time became inadequate. In 1963, the University decided to build the beautiful new edifice now standing. In order to have ample space the original brick building was moved back several hundred feet, and both buildings have been subsequently used for the Woodrow Wilson School. Over the entrance of the original building is inscribed the name of Edwin S. Corwin.

CARLOS BAKER
1909 –

I first met this distinguished educator and author in 1953, the year of my election as President of the Nassau Club. It has been the custom for years to have a prominent speaker at each Wednesday luncheon. This is a highlight of the week, and all Wednesday luncheons are well attended. Among other things, the president meets the speaker prior to the luncheon and, with some of the trustees, enjoys a private half hour of socializing before introducing him to the members.

In June of 1953, Carlos Baker was scheduled to speak on the subject, "My Interpretation of Hemingway's *The Old Man and the Sea.*" He delivered a penetrating discussion of this popular work. My introduction was brief, since he was so well-known. After he spoke for the allotted half hour, the audience asked for more. During the ensuing hour that he spoke, one could hear a pin drop.

From this point on, I saw Carlos Baker infrequently, but our meetings were cordial. He flattered me four years later, when he returned as a speaker at the Club, in requesting that I introduce him once again.

Carlos' book, *Ernest Hemingway, A Life Story,* was published in 1969, and remained on the best sellers' list for a number of weeks. I helped him ever so slightly on Ernest Hemingway, but he was kind enough to include my name, among many others who had been helpful, in the book's acknowledgment.

To have known Carlos Baker has been a great privilege. The following article from the "Alumni Album of Dartmouth," his alma mater, describes more fully his many achievements:

"One of the major literary events of the year took place in April when Scribner's brought out *Ernest Hemingway: A Life Story,* the product of seven years of research and writing by Carlos Baker, '32. From the time Hemingway's publisher announced that Baker would be the author of this authorized biography there has been an unusual amount of talk about this book (750 pages, 100 illustrations, $10 the copy), and a very large sale is expected. The biography was the Book-of-the-Month Club selection for April.

"Although Carlos Baker, who is Woodrow Wilson Professor of Literature at Princeton, corresponded with Hemingway for ten years prior to the famous writer's death in 1961, the two men never met. Baker's 1952 book, *Hemingway: The Writer as Artist* was the first full-length critical study of Ernest Hemingway's work and was mainly responsible for launching their friendship by mail. After the writer's death, the cooperation of his widow, Mary Hemingway, was essential to the preparation of the definitive biography and this was fully given. 'Mary was very good in giving me free access to all her husband's papers and to her own diary as well,' Baker has stated. 'She never attempted to influence my judgments, although at her request I omitted some material she wanted to reserve for an autobiography she is contemplating.'

"Taking on the writing of the definitive story of this great American author was no small challenge, but in many ways Carlos Baker was the perfect man for the job. To his unsurpassed knowledge of Hemingway's works he added the advantages of being an experienced literary scholar and a novelist himself. His two novels, also published by Scribner's, are *A Friend in Power* (1958) and *The Land of Rumbelow* (1963). In addition to a book about Shelley and a collection of his own poetry, *A Year and A Day* (1963), he had edited eleven other books, two of them related to Hemingway, has written many literary essays and reviews, and . . . has been lecturer at Oxford and a Guggenheim Fellow. The town of Princeton knows him as a many-sided citizen and has saluted him as its 'Man of the Year.' No less than Ernest Hemingway, his favorite subject, Carlos Baker has been an activist all his life."

On January 2, 1963, I decided to merge with the excellent firm of Clark, Dodge and Co., Inc. I became a Vice-President and opened a Princeton office for them. A member of the New York Stock Exchange with an excellent advisory department and a splendid research organization, the firm had been very successful for many years.

There were several reasons that motivated this move. My son, Harland, Jr., who had been with me for fourteen years, decided to go into the educational field, and his going left quite a gap. Also, I had reached an age when I felt that my clients deserved protection against my eventual retirement.

Clark, Dodge did a substantial brokerage business, but I had a definite understanding that my time would be devoted entirely to the

Investment Advisory accounts. About two years prior to the merger, I had employed Leighton Laughlin to assist in handling these accounts. Leighton, his three brothers, and his parents had all been clients of mine for several years. He was a man of great ability and I was fortunate in obtaining his services. He was also quite flexible, and with the merger with Clark, Dodge, I asked him to take over the responsibility of the brokerage business. He agreed to take this assignment, and soon he had Arthur Morgan on his staff – Arthur being another very high-grade man.

As time went on, they employed three additional men, and together created a substantial brokerage business. In the meantime, I carried out my original plan to devote all of my time to Investment Counsel. I was assisted by the firm's Advisory Department in New York, and the arrangement worked out very satisfactorily.

In December, 1969, I decided to withdraw from Clark, Dodge. Again, I was motivated by my age and a desire to take it easier, as well as to be able to devote more time to writing. I turned over many of my advisory clients to Clark, Dodge, but retained ten or twelve in order to keep my interests in the business. I now have a lovely little office at One Palmer Square, facing Nassau Hall and the beautiful Princeton campus. I conduct business under my own name and with an extremely capable secretary, Mrs. Grace Metz, who has been with me many years.

So, at my advanced age, I again find myself in business independently, and in many ways it is a satisfying feeling. Entering my fifty-second year in the Investment Counseling field, I intend to proceed in this manner as long as I am physically and mentally able. There is an adage which says, "When one has reached the age where he can watch his step, he is too old to go anywhere." I am not in that position yet.

CHAPTER ELEVEN

WALL STREET UPHEAVAL

The 1969-1970 bear market reached its low point on May 26, 1970, with the Dow-Jones Industrial Average at 631.11. One year prior to this it had been at 930. The Average did not remain at the May level too long, although a sustained rally failed to occur immediately. After the low point, the market gradually moved forward, and by January, 1971, had reached the 870 level. A change downward in interest rates helped, and many investors felt that the prior reaction had been too severe.

The drop in interest rates beginning in late 1970 was phenomenal. The prime rate, which had been 8 1/2% a year ago, fell to 6% by January, 1971. Later in the year it went to 5 1/2%. Naturally, bond prices rose dramatically. Many investors had shifted from stocks throughout 1970 in order to benefit from the fantastic yields available in bonds, but the tide finally turned, helping give the stock market a shot in the arm. An example of high yields, the U. S. Treasury sold some 7-year notes in February, 1970 yielding 8% – the highest rate for a government issue since 1788.

For many years there had been a feeling among investors that the New York Stock Exchange was run by a few individuals as a private club. There existed a small group of influential and wealthy men who made their own rules and would brook no interference. The SEC has changed this to some extent in recent years, but reforms did not go nearly far enough. When the 1969-1970 bear market suddenly descended on Wall Street, it served to bring out the many weaknesses that existed. Wall Street remains confronted with an accumulation of very crucial issues that have to be faced and resolved.

The last three New York Stock Exchange Presidents, Emil Schram, Keith Funston and Robert W. Haack, tried valiantly to put through needed reforms, but the Board of Governors resisted their efforts and stubbornly refused to make the necessary changes. Mr. Haack, elected President in 1967, called for an administrative restructuring of the Exchange to deal more effectively with its many problems. In the Fall of 1970 he had the courage, without consulting his directors, to recommend sweeping changes in the commission rate structure. He was immediately denounced by several of his governors, but one or two upheld his position and other prominent men in the field of finance applauded him.

Following the most serious financial upheaval since the Depression, Wall Street needed to make reforms in the following areas:

1. *A new commission rate structure* for security transactions. No overall adjustment of commission rates had been made for thirteen years.

2. *Elimination of inefficiencies* in the back offices of stock exchange firms – an important contributing factor to the recent financial crisis. Average cost of handling a single transaction has more than doubled since 1958 – from about $25.00 to nearly $59.00. From 1968 through 1970 clerical cost soared more than 80% and cost of equipment jumped 150%.

3. *New capital structure* – more capital and capital that is liquid. The problem of capital and where to get it was one of the major problems facing the industry as it emerged from the darkest period since 1929. For several years discussions have been going on with the SEC and the New York Stock Exchange that would permit member firms to go public. Finally in April 1970, permission was granted. Donaldson, Lufkin & Jenrette, Inc. offered shares in its firm at $15 per share. This firm threatened to quit the exchange if it could not go public. They sold 800,000 shares. Market conditions were bad and the stock sold as low as $5. In October of 1971 it was selling around $11.

Merrill Lynch went public in June 1971 and was the first Big Board member firm to have its shares listed on the Exchange. Stock was offered at $28, went as high as $42 and in October, 1971, was selling at about $37. Benefiting from general improvement in Wall Street, Merrill Lynch reported a first half profit of over $40 million, up 160% from the year earlier.

Bache & Co., second in size only to Merrill Lynch, sold 2.5 million shares at $16 in September of 1971. One month later it was about $13.50 bid over-the-counter.

CBWL-Hayden, Stone Inc. went public late in 1971, selling one million shares at $12.50.

Several other firms such as Dean Witter & Co., Paine, Webber, Jackson and Curtis and Reynolds & Co. have announced intentions to go public.

It is too early to predict how much of this kind of financing can be done by member firms. To a great extent it will depend on market conditions.

4. *Possible merging* of the New York and American Stock

Exchanges. In *The Wall Street Journal* on Wednesday, November 16, 1970, Ralph S. Saul, President of the American Stock Exchange, commented on the industry's burdens with confusing systems and rules. "The nation's stock exchanges and other securities industry components are not effectively solving the industry's several problems," he said.

Wall Street has a way of surging from euphoria to despondency. Just over a dozen months prior to this time the securities industry had been expanding with reckless abandon and speculation was rampant. And yet 1970 was to witness many forced liquidations, failures, and mergers among New York Stock Exchange members. These developments demonstrated the clearly deplorable mismanagement of many brokerage firms.

Following the great speculative orgy of 1968-1969 and thereafter, more than 100 brokerage firms had to go out of business, with hundreds of branch offices closed and thousands of people discharged. The securities industry has truly undergone a radical transformation and many more changes will take place in the months ahead. Fortunately, the public has not realized how much was at stake in keeping Wall Street above water, and how persistently crisis after crisis dogged the industry for a much longer period than anyone likes to admit. A few near-catastrophes might be mentioned to shed some light on the chaotic situation.

Hayden, Stone Inc., long regarded as a pillar in the securities industry, encountered problems in the early stages of this upheaval. To illustrate a case of imprudent expansion, this firm increased its branch offices from nine in 1959 to eighty-two in mid-1968. Registered representatives increased at even a greater ratio. This overexpansion naturally caught up, and a real crisis developed. The organization lost $9.2 million in the first seven months of 1970 on the heels of $10.9 million lost in 1969. Finally, a merger with other firms was consummated on September 11, 1970, and a real disaster was averted. Wall Street breathed more easily, but not for long. It has finally been revealed that among the company's capital assets was a sizable amount of Four Seasons Nursing, which, as described in *Chapter Seven,* had gone into bankruptcy some months earlier.

Following this near-catastrophe other cracks began to surface. Goodbody & Co., one of the largest and best-known firms, had expanded much too fast, with back office work hopelessly snarled. Although its executives continued to deny difficulties, it became obvious that this firm was in deep trouble. By this time the Special

Trust Fund, established by the New York Stock Exchange members to protect customers from insolvent firms, was totally exhausted; there was no protection left for the 250,000 clients of Goodbody. Exchange President Haack said that if Goodbody failed there could be no real future for the industry.

In desperation member firms agreed to put up $30 million and prevailed on Merrill, Lynch, Pierce, Fenner & Smith to take over this troubled firm as a wholly-owned subsidiary. Thus another crisis was narrowly averted, with Merrill Lynch taking a courageous step to save what would have been one of the most profound financial breakdowns in Wall Street history.

Yet still another shock was in the making. Rumors soon began to spread that Francis I. duPont & Co. – approximately the size of Goodbody – was in trouble. In July of 1970 there had been one of the largest mergers in Wall Street history, with F. I. duPont joining Hirsch & Co., Glore Forgan Staats, Inc. Although drastic cutbacks were made, the merger unfortunately came just as the market sank into the summer doldrums, with volume at an extremely low level. Revenues for all firms reached a perilously depressed level. It had been generally assumed that the duPont interests in Wilmington, Delawáre, would always protect this name to the limit. But even the wealthiest of people can become weary of backing a losing horse. In late November a solution was finally found. H. Ross Perot, Chairman of the fabulously successful Electronic Data Systems, Inc., was prevailed upon to make a $10 million loan to this financially troubled firm. A few months later it was necessary for Mr. Perot to add an additional $40 million. Once again Wall Street was saved from a disaster that would have been cataclysmic.

Subsequently, on December 21, 1970, the Senate passed a bill creating a government agency to protect *investors,* for the first time in history. Known as S.I.P.C. – Securities Investor Protection Corporation – it is perhaps the most significant legislation, other than the forming of the SEC, of the twentieth century. It provides an advance up to $50,000 per customer in the event of the liquidation of an S.I.P.C. member, and is backed by a $1 billion line of credit from the Federal Treasury. The cataclysmic decline of the previous months, with all the wreckage it created, finally gave birth to something good.

Bear markets like the 1969-1970 crash not only affect New York Stock Exchange firms. Reverberations spread to the entire nation, taking their toll with individual investors, mutual funds, trust funds, pension funds, and corporations. Like a stone cast into a small pond, the ripples do not stop until they have spread gradually over the entire surface of the water. Hundreds of examples could be cited where the drastic decline in the stock market brought anguish to corporations and individuals. I shall attempt to describe one or two of the more startling ones.

Probably the one most surprising was the bankruptcy of Lammon duPont Copeland Jr., great-great-grandson of the founder of the enormous duPont company. Strange that this happened shortly before the story broke on the troubled Francis I. duPont, Glore Forgan Staats firm, although there was no relationship. Young Copeland, whose father had been President and later Chairman of the huge duPont (E.I.) de Nemours and Company, struck out on his own several years ago and succeeded in putting together a colossal jerry-built empire that eventually collapsed early in November, 1970. Bankruptcy papers revealed liabilities of a staggering $55 million and possible assets of $25 to $30 million (many of the assets of doubtful value) from some hundred creditors, including banks and individuals. He listed various trusts as assets; it has since been revealed that these trusts cannot be touched by creditors.

PENN CENTRAL COMPANY

Now comes one of the most fantastic and bizarre stories of the twentieth century. Formed in February, 1968, by merging New York Central Railroad into Pennsylvania Railroad – and including the bankrupt N.Y., New Haven and Hartford in January 1969 – it created a gigantic system covering 24,000 miles of road. It took Stuart Saunders, formerly President of the Norfolk and Western Railroad, and his associates several years to obtain approval of the I.C.C. and various other agencies, and finally consummate what was hailed as the greatest accomplishment in railroad history.

In his many years as President of the Norfolk and Western, Stuart Saunders had gained a reputation as the greatest genius in the railroad industry – and rightfully so. With virtually all debt retired, this coal-carrying system became the most prosperous railroad complex in the nation. Generous dividends were paid, and holders of the common stock fared very well. Today Mr. Saunders undoubtedly wishes he had remained with Norfolk and Western. But like many successful men he became too ambitious, which paved the way to his downfall and the debacle that followed.

The merger was hailed on all sides as a great achievement, with prospects for large earnings and a substantial growth potential. It was received with such enthusiasm that the stock reached a figure of $80. By the early part of 1971 it was selling at $5.

Optimistic statements were issued from management and within investment circles. But from the beginning unseen problems were inherent. The many hidden weaknesses of the gigantic enterprise started to appear in early 1969, but we were well into 1969 before many of them were revealed. This year ended with very meager earnings, compared to $2.50 per share in 1968.

By May of 1970 the situation was desperate, and a bankruptcy petition was filed on June 21. A dazed and bewildered public suddenly realized that one of the greatest swindles of the twentieth century had left them with tremendous losses and with slim hopes of recouping very much.

To attempt to enumerate all of the contributing factors to this fiasco would require volumes. A few of them were:

1. Too many high-salaried executives.
2. Far too many workmen on the payroll. Extravagant promises were made to labor.
3. High interest rates.
4. Jealousy between workers in the N.Y. Central and the Penn Railroads, resulting in friction.
5. Exaggerated estimates for earnings from certain subsidiary holdings – especially the vast real estate holdings in Florida, Texas and California.

In December of 1970 the House Committee on Banking and Currency had this to say about Penn Central's investment in Executive Jet Aviation Co. "There was deceit, irresponsibility and squandering of assets. It was one of the saddest – and at times one of the most sordid – pictures of the American business community that has ever been revealed." Penn Central had lost practically all of its $21 million investment.

Penn Central lost $252 million for the first ten months of 1970. Losses for the same period the year before had been $57 million. Early in 1971, Great Southwest Corp., a Texas affiliate, announced that it had written down its consolidated net worth by over $107 million. Certainly the entire Penn Central picture appeared hopeless.

Securing capital funds is one problem facing New York Stock Exchange firms. Already cited is the $10 million that Mr. Perot placed in the duPont, Glore Forgan Staats firm, with indications that more might be available. In addition to this gesture by business to provide funds, Drexel, Harriman Ripley recently revealed that Firestone Tire and Rubber Company had invested $10 million dollars in its firm. Indications were that this amount might be considerably increased, pending approval of the SEC.

Perhaps enough has been said about weaknesses recently prevailing in some New York Stock Exchange firms, but a few other items of interest might be mentioned. At the height of the speculative orgy, expansion was the keynote. We have already cited Hayden, Stone's increase in offices from nine to eighty-two in a period of nine years. Several other firms followed the same pattern. In Wall Street many firms doubled and tripled office space. Builders anxious to swim with the tide built newer and higher buildings; as a result, rents skyrocketed. At one point of this frenzied atmosphere prime office space was being rented up to $13 per square foot with 5-to 10-year leases. Then came the crash. This space is now available for about one-half that amount, and there is plenty of it available.

In the Spring of 1970, a membership seat on the New York Stock Exchange sold for $130,000, although the price had recovered to around $225,000 by Sept. 1971.

An article in *The Wall Street Journal* on Friday, October 9, 1970 stated that only twelve of the top thirty-two Big Board firms were in the black on commission business during the 1969 profit squeeze. But it is not fair to condemn all firms, for there were many that kept their houses clean and made money consistently. For example, although Merrill, Lynch, Pierce, Fenner and Smith, Inc., the nation's largest securities firm, lost an estimated $5.7 million on its brokerage operations in 1969, the company reported that it still rolled up $32.8 million net profit from all sources.

Figures also disclose that the four most profitable firms of 1968 all repeated at the top of the 1969 list – Salomon Brothers, Goldman Sachs & Co., Donaldson, Lufkin and Jenrette, Inc., and White, Weld & Co.

Is it surprising that there has been an upheaval in Wall Street? Investors are now wondering if the worst is over. Will we see more failures? Are there any more situations similar to Penn Central? Will New York Stock Exchange firms put their houses in order and establish rules and regulations and procedures that will protect the investor? These and other questions cannot be answered with too much assurance. We must hope that the experiences of the past few years will bring home to Wall Street, to bankers and to business, the inescapable fact that speculative excesses can bring only trouble. With the help of the SEC, Congress and Wall Street, measures are being implemented to prevent another period such as prevailed during this 1969 and 1970 bear market.

CHAPTER TWELVE

WHITHER GOEST?

What success I have enjoyed in this business arises from a fairly fixed permanent policy – a theme that I have emphasized with little deviation. It was my conviction, especially from 1930 on, that our nation possessed tremendous wealth and that our Gross National Product would gradually increase, along with spendable income, dividends – and stock values. I therefore advised my clients to place emphasis on quality and to keep a long-term perspective; that is, not to be influenced by short-term swings in the market. Today I have some clients who hold IBM at 10 and General Motors at 5. And despite the big decline in the market during the past year and a half, many of the stocks purchased twenty-five to thirty years ago still show a handsome profit.

To attempt to predict what the stock market will do in the coming year is difficult indeed. That we as a nation are faced with many serious problems there can be little doubt. I have attempted to put some of these problems in their proper perspective. To sum up the most serious ones: How successful will we be in withdrawing from Vietnam? In controlling prices and wages and halting the inflationary spiral? How long can we see money rates lowered and will they stabilize? How successful will we be in assimilating the Negro into our society? If we had a statesman in the White House dedicated to solving these problems and big enough to realize that partisan politics must be thrown aside if they are to be solved, I could be more optimistic.

This nation still has vast resources and great wealth. We are capable of solving our problems with determination and with the right leadership. But as I look ahead I am inclined to think that my fifty-second year in this business will be a difficult one. As always, some companies and some industries will do better than others, and the Investment Counselor and the investor must concentrate on attempting to locate these situations. Over 100 months have gone by since the initial upturn in business experienced in 1961. This is an unprecedented record – the longest period of generally rising business this country has known. Today our Gross National Product is at a very high level. So is spendable income; and unemployment is only 6%.

But there is a feeling of uncertainty in the populace. What is behind this uneasiness? For the most part, it is due to the absence of planning on the part of our national leaders. Our government is attempting to turn around an unacceptably large rise in the general price level, accounted for by an unfinanced war superimposed upon a sensitive economy.

On June 3, 1969, I attended a meeting of the Board of Directors of a corporation with a sizable investment portfolio. As Chairman, I asked each Director to give his views on the market. They were all reasonably cautious, but felt that our 15% in sixty-day commercial paper, 10% in convertible bonds, and 75% in common stocks was sound. I purposely waited until the last, and rather surprised my fellow Directors by saying that I was quite bearish. The Dow-Jones Industrial Average was then 930.78. I made the prediction that we would see it at 750 before the end of the year, and possibly at 700 before July 1, 1970. One of the Directors made a small bet with me that the 750 figure would not be seen in 1969. I lost by a small margin, because the low was 766 in December. In May, 1970, it went as low as 631.11.

I purposely had my views placed in the documented minutes. My reasons for this gloomy prediction were:

1. Our very high interest rates.
2. Danger of wage and price controls.
3. Continuation of hostilities in Vietnam.
4. Declining corporate profits.

What, then, is in store for 1972 and beyond? As commented in *Chapter Five,* "When attempting to chronicle the great cyclical swings in our stock market, one should remember that the psychology of investors constitutes perhaps fifty percent of the factors at work. Economic and monetary factors are important, but it is *stock market sentiment* that drives markets to extremes – both up and down."

The market demonstrated a very substantial recovery from 631 in May, 1970, to 920 by September of 1971. Confidence of investors had been restored for several reasons:

1. Formation of the S.I.P.C.
2. Lower interest rates
3. President Nixon's promises to get us out of Vietnam
4. His proposed trip to Peking

5. Attempts to alleviate our imbalances of payments and trade by means of the temporary surcharge, wage-price freeze and dollar flotation.

Undoubtedly, several of President Nixon's recommendations made August 15, 1971, carried bullish implications. But one must remember that he was compelled to take this course when he finally grasped the gravity of our situation and the fact that his economic game plan was striking out. Our dollar had been increasingly weak for several months. Our balance of payments deficit had sunk to a dangerous level; according to figures published through mid-August, some $22 billion more dollars flowed out of the country than came in. Imports exceeded exports by a growing margin. We were still spending billions on the Vietnam War and other billions on space exploration. Both of these last two items demand financing that returns no productive good to our economy. Guns, jet fighters, bombs and space ships cannot be used to build schools, hospitals, provide mass transit, build houses or eliminate ghettoes.

Will all of our problems be cured even if President Nixon's recommendations are carried out, or are they merely a palliative that incited our hopes? All sane-thinking citizens know that most of our troubles stem from the foolhardy fiscal irresponsibility of our government. Is anyone naive enough to think that bureaucratic Washington is going to go into reverse suddenly, balance our budget, stop the profligate waste and return to sanity? Will our Congress and the Executive Branch of our government have the courage to make the needed reforms? I for one do not believe it.

Ponder on these figures. In 1900 our national debt was $1.4 billion. The New Deal increased it to $55 billion. Now we have passed the $400 billion figure with no end in sight. Interest on our national debt is $20 billion – more than our entire debt in 1932. Our military budget is $70 billion a year.

By September of 1971, the majority of the money managers in Wall Street were bullish. This includes mutual funds with assets of $50 billion, investment trusts, pension fund managers, advisory services, trust department heads, and members of the New York Stock Exchange.

Once again the signs are ominous. Just as Wall Street "has a way of surging from euphoria to despondency," the reverse can be set in motion and gain momentum. If we should enter a period of increasing speculation, we are apt to lay the groundwork for another Wall Street

Upheaval. To attempt to pinpoint the time is not easy, because these speculative orgies always go too far.

On the other hand, we are still faced with the realities of inflation, our soaring national debt, the conclusion of our Vietnam commitment, near-bankruptcy of several of our largest cities, environmental pollution, continuing racial problems, and the chaotic welfare program.

A political pundit has recently come up with an idea that may be having its influence now. As he put it, "The stock market is a political thermometer. It measures the hot or cold state of mind of literally millions of shareholders. They either have confidence enough to invest their money in the future of various companies or they don't. A look at the charts will show that third years of every recent administration have been periods of rising stock prices." This was true in the administrations of Truman, Eisenhower, Kennedy, Johnson, and came to pass in the same way under Nixon. This factor, along with those mentioned, may account for the substantial recovery – on heavy volume – in the market during late 1970 into 1971.

We might pause for a moment to consider the rally that followed the debacle of October and November, 1929. A rally of more than 50% occurred from the November low to an April, 1930 high. Following that recovery, the market then staged another and more precipitous decline. Most authorities, however, feel that the situation today is not comparable to 1929. Our problems are undeniably serious, but some steps are being taken in an attempt to solve them.

Do we have the will, the determination, and the resolve to solve them? I wish I knew the answer to the question of our future economic state of health. But this is not the first time in fifty-one years of Investment Counseling that I have been in this predicament.

In closing, I can express a definite opinion on four very important matters that will be of great concern to all investors in the years ahead. 1) We can expect regular increases in taxes – local, state and federal; 2) gradual but continuing erosion of the dollar will make protection against inflation of utmost importance; 3) more than ever, investors will need to seek the best professional advice obtainable; 4) recent dramatic developments, and others still to come, will have a profound effect on our markets during the next ten years.

Just as buying a particular stock can result in rewards or disappointing losses, the choice of an Investment Counselor can be fortunate or devastatingly costly. For there are at least as many kinds of counselors – qualified or amateur, conscientious or only self-seeking

– as there are stocks to buy. Prudent judgment in discerning the difference is certainly the crucial criterion when placing your future financial life in someone's hands.

When that is accomplished, *off you go* – and Good Luck!